To Louis
you all

GW01066122

THE
ART OF MENTAL MUSCLE:

Using Life's Challenges To Build Internal Strength And Other Qualities.

TONY PRYCE

Grounded Vision

THE
ART OF MENTAL MUSCLE:

Using Life's Challenges To Build Internal Strength And Other Qualities.

Published by Grounded Vision

First Edition

TONY PRYCE 2006

Tony Pryce asserts the moral right to be identified as the author of this work.

ISBN 0-9550861-0-8

Printed and bound in Great Britain by Biddles Ltd

Published By Grounded Vision
Artwork and internal design by Tony Pryce
Cover design by Shahed Miah (connect2shahed@yahoo.co.uk)

©

Author Biography

Tony Pryce is a primary and secondary school teacher who holds a degree in Psychology and Philosophy, as well as a Post Graduate Certificate in Education (PGCE) in English. The Art Of *Mental Muscle* grew out of the programmes he would construct for people suffering from depression, low self-esteem and general life complaints, as well as a philosophical interest in martial arts and physical development.

He has written two stage plays to date: *Haven Can Wait* and *The Spirit of Robeson.* He has also written a workbook, aimed at increasing the self-esteem of children, entitled: *In Your Mind's Eye.*

Acknowledgments

Thank you to: Veena Stephenson for giving me that enthusiastic push along the road when these writings were forming themselves into a book: Russell Miller for adopting the philosophy whilst I was still in the middle of the journey. A huge thank you is due to Judith Cross. You were there to welcome me with open arms and much cheer as I began to cross the finishing line. Your feedback; the time you gave to proof-reading, and your ideas were a real blessing; especially your renaming of this work. Additionally, your support, assistance and encouragement has been beyond any writer's dream. John and Roger: thanks, for sorting out the computer which has enhanced my writing. Thank you, Natalie, for helping to keep me going in general. Thanks Shahed, for giving up your time in order to find the right printer and design the jacket for the book. Thanks sis (Bella) for your efforts in also trying to see these words incarnate into book form.
Thanks are also due to Stephen Levey: for the generous loan of your proofreading skills.

No person is an island so special mention to Chiatulah, Mama, Rosie, Rhoda, Sam Theresa, Hubie, Jackie and Trevor, Arrosane, Rex, Peter, Anesha, Nyan, Philip, Olivia, Kerry, Wayne, Ayesha, Phil S. and the Northern Soul crowd.

Thanks to everyone who has ever placed obstacles in my path. You have forced me to dig deep and rise to a challenge.

To Judith "Darshie" Cross:

Your nurturing and support of the human spirit knows no bounds. More than any person I know, you always try to make other people's dreams come true. Your own courageous stance with regard to the battles you continue to face is truly inspiring.

And
To all those who would fight for something better.

Contents

Chapter 4

The Law Of Progressive Resistance

Chapter 5

Muscles Worth Developing

Introduction

Using Life's Challenges

"When you say 'yes' to a 'no' the 'no' becomes smaller until it is a 'yes'."

Dr Dhyan Sutorius

The mind is an extraordinarily powerful tool. It is responsible for some of the most remarkable events, spectacles, occurrences and achievements the world has ever known. It has brought us destruction on the one hand, yet innovative cures for major diseases on the other. It has helped to subject people to major acts of brutality and yet sublime acts of beauty and compassion. Whilst we stand at a crossroads between ways of being that could either secure or harm the planet, the mind's potential is both our means of salvation as well as our passport to further ill. *The Art Of Mental Muscle is* my humble attempt at aiding the process of helping to keep the mind trekking along a positive route.

With the rapid pace of technological change thrown into the mix, the world today can be a strange, lonely and confusing place. Despite events worthy of celebration, such as the end of apartheid in South Africa, and the crumbling of other regimes, sometimes the world just narrowly misses the next pitfall.

Often carried on the back of developments such as these, as effortlessly as pollen hitching a ride on the back of a bee, are insecurity and crisis. They get blown around and dispersed by whatever political and social breeze happens to be taking shape.

These mischievous twins are not necessarily bad, as long as their arrival is used as an opportunity for reflection, renewal and change, for the better. In fact, according to aspects of Chinese philosophy the notion of crisis in life is that it is not a one-way dead-end street whose end product is a wall built of stress and trauma. On the contrary, crisis is a path with a signpost marked *Opportunity*. It is this idea that has framed the vision of *The Art Of Mental Muscle*.

At an individual level it is plain to see that for some us life throws up many a spectre which, all too often, we are too afraid to look at. It is almost as though we feel that our problems will immobilise us, psychologically, in medusa-like fashion. We often rush around busily, with our heads down, which affords us the perfect excuse for not looking. What we don't see, we reason, can't have any power over us. If we just continue to move around quickly enough then whatever is pursuing us may just run out of breath and collapse on the floor in a heap.

However, you need to look life's events squarely in the face in order to have some sort of influence or impact on them. When you can't do this then you often find that it is at this point that life's events have the most power over you, and consequently, do the most damage.

Courage, and other qualities, are needed both to be able to face up to life and make necessary changes to both yourself and the world, where necessary. It goes without saying then that tools are needed which can enable you to gain qualities such as courage, confidence, perseverance and any other quality that can help in this regard. It is from this point of view that I have written this book.

The central idea put forward in this work is that the mind, and other facets of it involving consciousness, awareness and the ability to process knowledge etc, is analogous to muscle. Therefore, many of the ideas for training physical muscle, as I shall go on to demonstrate, are applicable to the mind.

With mind, as with any muscle, there is the potential for growth. For example, we readily acknowledge that people can increase their sense of knowledge, wisdom and understanding about the world as a result of their experiences. The philosophy behind that of education is that education encourages the growth of the mind. We also learn skills, adapt to circumstances and new conditions as well as increase reaction times to performing tasks, with consistent practice.

Another factor that acted as a spur to my writing this book was an incident that happened to me during the course of my student days. For some reason, unknown to me at the time, I began to enter a phase where I began to feel quite low, mentally. This state manifested itself in a strange fashion: I found it hard to open my mail. I noticed how this occurrence didn't take place overnight, it happened a little at a time: The development of the mood, in other words, was systematic.

The fact that I couldn't open the envelopes stood for something. It was symbolic, but regardless of what it stood for I came to notice how much it was like the type of problem that can beset muscles. They can atrophy, through lack of use or injury, which can then lead them to handle less and less of a load.

I also realised that, in order to heal myself, I didn't necessarily have to delve into what not being able to open the envelopes meant. I could simply tackle the problem by merely confronting it in its symbolic form. I treated it like a weight-lifting exercise for the mind and gave myself an ever-increasing load to handle: It worked; I became stronger, mentally.

Human beings are very interesting in that they live life in both a real and symbolic form. That is, events and occurrences in the world can often come to represent, mirror or stand for what is happening inwardly. For example, a man finds himself getting excessively angry with a stranger, out of proportion to the event that should only have prompted minor irritation. On reflection he finds that the over-reaction was due to the fact that the stranger reminded him of a cruel boss he used to work for. Symbolically, he treated the stranger in the manner in which he would have liked to have treated his boss. Therapies, such as Psychoanalysis and Psychotherapy, are founded on the unpicking of such rich symbolism.

Sometimes, you only need to tackle the symbolic form of a problem, for a corresponding shift towards a healthy state to take place in the psyche.

Thinking of the mind as a muscle serves a number of useful functions. In the first place it will provide you with a way of conceptualising mental growth. Secondly, it offers a visual metaphor which can help you become stronger with respect to certain psychological qualities that you might wish to develop. Thirdly, conceptualising mind as muscle allows you to think about the shape you are in, mentally, and, if you so choose, the shape you would prefer to be in.

It then follows that you can set goals for yourself in order to achieve this aim. Finally, thinking of the mind as a muscle will provide your imagination with something to work on, as well as providing a framework upon which you can hang a vision of change. However, this is not the whole picture. The similarity with which mind has been compared with muscle has never been lost on people, even if unconsciously.

It is for no idle reason, as I shall go on to outline, that during the course of everyday conversations people talk in terms of having "burdens to carry" or "sharing loads" and other such phrases. However, at the same time the idea of the mind being a muscle has never been made truly explicit either. Perhaps this is because of the peculiar philosophical tradition in the West of separating the mind from the body.

Perhaps there is one area where we can readily appreciate the idea of mind as a muscle and that is with regard to memory training. Harry Lorayne, writing in *How to Develop a Super-power- Memory* makes the case for memory itself as a kind of substrata of muscle that can be trained and developed. Insofar as a true test for the presence of muscle is that muscle has both the capacity for expansion as well as the ability to handle greater loads then memory certainly fits this picture. Lorayne writes:

> I believe that the more you remember, the more you can remember. The memory, in many ways, is like a muscle. A muscle must be exercised and developed in order to give proper service and use; so must the memory. You can be taught to have a trained memory just as you can be taught anything else.[1]

The only thing you need to start a process of training the memory, he acknowledges, is "interest." This self-development programme is not dissimilar in its requirements.

It is also of interest to note the similarity between exercising the body, through the use of weights etc, and exercising the mind by way of learning, accommodating and adapting to new experiences. For instance, let us consider the use of repetition. Repetition plays a very important part in the building of physiological muscle. As any athlete will tell you it is an essential component. It is through steady and calculated repetition (of the use of weights for instance) that the muscle is worked to capacity, in order that muscular growth can be secured.

You can also see the importance of repetition in learning. Noel Entwistle: writing in *Understanding Classroom Learning* makes the link clear:

> Our everyday behaviour is full of chains of actions which are made automatic through repeated practice whether it is getting breakfast or driving the car. Efficient everyday living depends on making automatic a great deal of what we have learned by frequent repetition.[2]

Repetition of anything acts as a kind of reinforcement, and we know (from very early psychological experiments) that reinforcement works, like a glue, to fix new behaviour, learning or attitudes in place. Reinforcement can run the range from basic repetition right through to encouragement and support.

There are a number of people who, for me, embody the spirit of what I see as the mental muscle philosophy or way of being. One of these was a dancer, who went by the name of Peg Leg Bates. He was a man who lost his leg quite early on during his adolescence. However, this was far from being a hindrance to him, as he didn't see the significance of this "loss" insofar as people usually interpret such incidents. In an account he gave of what happened he said that it was, "Just like stubbing my toe."

He just couldn't conceptualise what had happened to him as a problem, therefore it was not. He took up many sports including baseball, cycling, horse riding and swimming. In fact he went on to become a famous dancer who won many a competition. This had nothing to do with pity he exacted from others and everything to do with the fantastic dance style he created. Bates said of his style: "...I wanted to be so good; I wanted to surpass the two-legged dancers! And in a lot of cases I did." [3]

I will go on to demonstrate that just as muscle responds to resistance, in the form of weights etc, by growing, so too can mind grow through the studied use of life's resistance.

From the human mind's point of view, what precisely is this resistance? It is the very challenges to your will, desires, efforts and intentions both large and small, that confront you as part of your everyday life experiences. Whether such resistance is created by other people, yourself or is simply a by-product of nature's processes doesn't really matter. It is still resistance and therefore is of use to you from a mental muscle perspective.

The overcoming of or making use of resistance from a mental muscle perspective will be the wilful meeting of life's challenges rather than merely bumping into them accidentally, with all the chaos, fear and anxiety that this can entail. The distinction is an important one. It is one that is meant to signal your status as an active agent rather than a passive one.

Let's look at it another way: Imagine a scenario where you are about to lose the job you most cherish or, as in many cases, need. What do you feel, anxiety, debilitating fear or even terror? Now imagine the same scenario but this time you say to yourself; "I find the prospect of losing my job a worrying one but is there any benefit that I might I be able to gain from it, given the fact that I can do nothing to prevent the situation?"

The mere fact of being able to have the latter dialogue with yourself is more empowering because you are interacting positively with what has been thrown at you, and in the process challenging the fear that can leave you experiencing a type of psychological rigor mortis.

There is no reason why people in general shouldn't be able to think in this way about a whole range of obstacles that confront them. When you think about it there is no universal law, set down in a tablet of stone, which dictates the way you should react to a set of circumstances.

If you take a long hard look at the divergence of cultures around the world you will see that, collectively, people have a wide variety of emotional responses to incidents; suggesting that some responses are determined by nothing more than cultural heritage. The way indigenous Mexicans view and celebrate death is one example that springs to mind. On an individual basis people can differ markedly in their response to something such as a tragedy.

One of the times that people feel at their most depressed or insecure is when they feel both at the mercy of events that are affecting them and powerless to direct or play an active part in those events. This programme is designed to make you an active participant even when things are being done to you.

Many martial artists and health practitioners, such as acupuncturists, subscribe to a belief in a particular form of energy that may be of help to us here, which is called Qui, or in some areas as Ki (Chi). The concept of Chi originated in ancient China, but is also one shared by other cultures. It is generally believed that Chi is an invisible form of bodily energy, or life force if you like, that is responsible for generating health and vitality. Manipulation of Chi has formed the basis of health practices such as Acupuncture. It is thought that the flow of Chi can be inhibited and disrupted by anything ranging from poor posture and physical rigidity through to negative life experiences. The aim of practices such as Acupuncture is to restore the balance of Chi.

I see a similar thing in terms of mental muscle. The more you can learn to be open to all your experiences, claiming and recycling even the "negative" ones, the more you can develop a positive flow of mental energy, leading to the creation of a more powerful way of being.

Such a way of thinking should leave you in a better position to be able to develop a being that is less tense, anxious, depressed and therefore ill. Psychological Chi, to my mind, is a psychic river of positive emotional energy that enables and empowers you to face life with all its tests and trials. The reverse of this are powerful mental inhibitors that incapacitate both body and mind. Think, for instance, about the damage that can be caused to oneself and others when guilt becomes free from its moorings to reason and gets out of hand.

Sometimes you come across people who are never stopped by anything. No matter the obstacle, they manage to maintain the same boundless spirit and enthusiasm. The actor Paul Robeson springs to mind as just one of the many examples. In one of the areas in which I once worked, a story was brought to my attention about a woman who, after undergoing brutal treatment in her home country, became a topic of psychological study. This was because health professionals couldn't understand how she emerged out of her experience a well-balanced, smiling, individual. When confronted with people such as this, we are forced to entertain a question about precisely what kind of inner workings, attitude or philosophy allows them to be that type of person, and whatever it is, is it available to us all? I would say yes and developing mental muscle offers a way.

At times when you lack confidence you may not attempt something or carry out an activity for fear of being knocked back or of "failing" to achieve that which you wish to or set out to achieve. It can feel as though there is a brick wall in your path inhibiting you. There may as well be because the effect is just the same; a lack of progress. On the other hand if you ask the question; "What can I get out of this?" irrespective of the question; "Will I succeed?" then this can be enough to break down the imaginary brick wall which prevents you from moving forward in your life or pursuing a challenge.

This programme, as much as anything, is also about helping you to shift your perspective so that you can dare to confront the issues and events that you are afraid of confronting, amongst other things.

This mental muscle programme has action at its heart. We are creatures of action as well as thought. The more we act and repeat patterns of activity the more the mind draws on these actions and gives us feedback on the type of people that we are either becoming or have the potential to be. Action, in this respect, acts as a signpost that can help direct us.

There isn't always the time or the money, for that matter, for us to pick through or investigate, in detective-like fashion, the reasons why we act the way we do. This is especially the case when our action is against our greater interest. Sometimes we just need to act and change if that is what is called for.

Additionally, because the types of actions we perform are often symbolic of our inner status, and the way we feel about ourselves, then acting in a different way from a negative pattern we have established, for instance, can often be enough to change the relationship that we have both with and within ourselves. This is because it offers external confirmation of another way of being. For example, if, as a person lacking in confidence, you join a martial arts class and you progress to a stage where you can chop through fifty bricks in one go then it becomes very hard to perceive yourself as weak.

How many times have you seen populist films where the unwitting hero or heroine stands up against the bully, hits them with a knockout blow, looks at his or her fist as though in utter disbelief at his or her new found power, then proceeds to believe in themselves through the increased advantage of a raised self-esteem. Whilst it is true that life isn't the movies sometimes the movies are a lot like life, with life – to dust down a cliché – often appearing to be stranger than fiction. That is why this programme works, because as soon as you have made one inspired change to a situation, or yourself, that you might not otherwise have done, then you have demonstrated mental muscular growth.

This programme requires some degree of work. Just as an athlete can't accumulate muscle without systematic work nor can you develop mental muscle without systematic work. It is all too clear that people do not automatically grow knowledge-wise, or with respect to wisdom, merely by tripping over the challenges that life has left hanging around.

Similarly, it is not automatically the case that people build anatomical muscle by simply carrying a heavy load. Both wisdom and muscle power is mostly gained when sought and worked for. Just as for the athlete, training for muscular development, it is both the system and application of study that makes a difference in the end, no matter how great the raw talent or the potential.

There is a question as to whether we can always use what is thrown at us. Aren't there some things we just can't turn to our advantage? What about the death of a loved one? For now all I will say is that when my stepfather died I felt bitterly wounded. But what could I do? I couldn't bring him back. Yet, without feeling guilty about doing so, I got something from the resistance which the experience offered or should I say I took from it. I was able to see and absorb the importance and preciousness of people rallying round each other, people who had no great material riches but who gave of themselves, nonetheless.

I was able to put into perspective so much of the insignificance of material life. His moving on brought into focus how some people subordinate others to dead matter and fight over and kill for things; not really realising what they are killing off in themselves. The experience forced me to ask myself whether I do give as much love as I can. This is a precious insight when the idea of loving openly is often seen as out of fashion, in a world where anything that doesn't have a stock market value is seen as invalid.

I was able to see these things because I trained myself to look, to look for the gold in the base metal of experience. What else could I do? It was a loss so I might as well try to gain something. I certainly did.

There is a simple unavoidable truth about this life, and it is that pain is largely unavoidable. However, if pain is a long playing record accompanying us on this journey, then pleasure is its B side. One comes with the other. There is another truth though and that is no matter how negative or painful an experience is, there are always people who are able to flip it to the B side and make it positive. Consider this thought. If we had no capacity to feel hurt or pain then what would our lives really be like?

We actually know from medical studies that people who feel no sensations of pain often have a rough time of it. Why? The answer is that they don't know when they are causing themselves an injury. As contradictory as it may sound, perhaps there is more pain to be had, ultimately, from being able to feel no pain at all.

Before I go on to the main part of this work, I would like to start with an examination, in the next chapter, of a series of ideas that will form the philosophical basis or underpinning for this programme. If the mental muscle programme, in its entirety, is an engine, then in the next chapter the ideas discussed therein are the oil that provides the lubrication for the engine. It concerns itself with how various philosophical and psychological aspects of the way life often works, forms an important part of the total mental muscle way of tackling challenges that face you. This is part of a general build up of the programme.

Each concept, in successive chapters, is meant to be understood, thoroughly, in order that it can provide a foundation for understanding the programme in its entirety. Similarly, athletes don't just educate themselves about the specifics of their sport, or just the bodybuilding aspect but must grasp fundamental ideas, such as how parts of or all of the body works, the effect of nutrition on the body, the importance of psychology and when to rest etc.

I would like to close this introduction by leaving the last word to Doreen Trust who, in this passage from her inspiring book, *Overcoming Disfigurement*, sums up exactly what this particular philosophy and programme, as well as its ultimate aim, is all about:

> Man has developed in order to develop his ever-growing, never-finished self against the resistance of an intractable and incomplete world; to overcome the hindrances within himself − apathy, indolence, greed, ignorance − amid, also in the people around him. He can treat these individuals as difficult, despicable or unlovable 'obstacles' or see them as opportunities for his talents of love, understanding and friendship. Man can adapt, resourcefully to material and spiritual difficulties.[4]

Chapter 1

Preparation For The Mental Athlete

Adversity is your greatest ally. Make friends with your misfortunes, otherwise you'll be forever angry.
Joel Hershman: Greenfingers

One of the main ideas behind the *Mental Muscle* programme is based on the following observation. When you look back on the past and reflect on some of the things that you hankered over, whether it is the job you wanted, the new house etc, failure to become successful in these areas and others might have caused you to harbour disappointments or bitter thoughts. However, if you make a close examination you might find that the failure of these things to come about led to better things being acquired when looked at within a long-term perspective.

Consider, for instance, the dancer who doesn't make the grade but as a result of taking another path becomes a renowned writer. What about the person who bemoans the fact that a close relationship has ended, only to stumble across the love of their life on another occasion. It is occurrences such as this that has given rise to the term: "A blessing in disguise." The converse is also true of course; sometimes that "heaven-sent" touch of luck can also prove to be the hand that makes for our undoing, further down the route which life takes us.

From this point of view, for the purposes of safeguarding psychological health, you might as well cultivate a certain attitude of mind, or create a psychological framework that is receptive to this feature of life. This is especially the case when you appreciate the sort of emotional power that thoughts can generate, particularly when they are negative. Disappointments, as far as the possibilities for consciousness is concerned, can become less a brick wall blocking your path than a doorway filled with the promise of, at the very least, an adventure. This leads to the following conclusions:

1) Not every event labelled "bad" or a "failure" that happens to you is necessarily to your detriment. It all depends on how you either view what has happened and/or make use of it.

2) You can make use of a situation's "failure" to deliver the expected benefits to lead to growth, and perhaps, greater emotional balance. For instance, such a positive perspective enables you to start to see an event as an opportunity; more of an open door than a closed one; more a beginning than an ending. This is especially the case when you appreciate, once again, that the results of a choice can lead anywhere in the long run. This understanding is central to this programme.

There is an old British film called *Laughter in Paradise* by Mario Zampi that illustrates the point brilliantly and comically. Made in 1951, this Ealing comedy tells the story of four potential heirs to a deranged uncle's will who are asked to participate in "out of character" activities. They are asked to do this in order to lay claim to part of the inheritance.

It is only on completion of the tasks which each has been given, and at some personal cost, that they are informed that that the uncle, far from leaving them a fortune as they had expected, has merely played a practical joke on them. Sorrowful and angry at first, at having being deceived, the film ends with the characters falling into a fit of uncontrollable laughter as they begin to acknowledge all the various ways in which they benefited from the exercise. The benefits for the characters included finding love and happiness; benefits they would not otherwise have obtained had they not taken the course of accepting the various challenges.

The film demonstrates two things of importance. The first is the potential benefits to be gained from accepting a challenge, even if you don't get the prize which the challenge offers. The second is that there is so much more that can be gained when you reflect, thoughtfully, on aspects of your life which you have consigned to the loss bin. In some cases this allows you to turn or recycle negative emotions and thoughts into more useful and positive ones. The characters' capacity to turn anger and sorrow into joy rested on their capacity to reflect on the benefits they had accumulated along the way. They saw the benefits when they looked closely enough for them.

Speaking personally about my own experience, God only knows how things would have turned out if I had indeed got the engineering job I sought desperately at the age of sixteen. This post hinged on my needing to have good maths skills which I didn't possess. That "failure" in maths, which I initially saw as a sign of inferiority, came to haunt me for many years.

On the other hand, I now believe that my sense of "failure" in this regard became a fillip to my developments in other areas, not only in areas such as the arts – becoming a Saxophone player – but also in terms of my understanding of life by way of reflection. I doubt whether I would have become a teacher if I had actually become that engineer I so wanted to become. On route to becoming a teacher I even tutored myself through a higher grade of maths, with a little help from my friends, than I could ever have envisaged tackling whilst I was a teenager. This achievement in turn also helped to boost my confidence enormously.

I cannot underestimate both the power inherent in learning to view life as a series of challenges from which something can be obtained as well as the benefits to be gained from so doing. For a start the fewer "problems" you have shelved at the back of your mind the greater the space you have for dealing with the things that you really want to or ought to pay attention to i.e. love, the pursuit of your goals and creativity etc. So it pays to transpose as many problems into challenges as possible.

There are two polarised attitudes of mind or forms of consciousness that relate to how people deal with life's events that I have given symbolical names to. The first type of mindset or form of consciousness I call **Water:** the second I call **Stick**. The former represents the ability to flow with life as it is and the latter represents the inability to do so. There are of course all the other variations in-between.

For the sake of argument, let's say that **Stick** as a material, (when compared to an element such as water) is fairly rigid. It is strong and is flexible, to a certain extent, but has its breaking point, obviously, when enough pressure is applied. A lot of us are rigid, psychologically speaking, in the same way.

One way that this rigidity manifests itself, is in our assumptions about how life should be. If life doesn't turn out the way that we envisage then we may snap (psychologically speaking) or become bitter which, because of its incapacitating effect, is merely a lesser version of snapping on the same slide-scale of experience.

We are not only rigid in this way. Sometimes we are rigid in the ideas we hold, either about ourselves, or about the world in general. This can take the form of holding a prejudicial view about someone, many people, or even holding a particularly unforgiving view of ourselves, which prevents us from making any progress to a more wholesome way of being. For instance, the fact that people feel bad about themselves, because of some past indiscretion, can turn into an endless round of self-criticism and self-punishing behaviour. This form of behaviour can put a break on healthy development.

Water as an element, on the other hand, flows with and in and around what is present, if given the slightest opportunity. It never seems capable of being trapped by anything. It has no ready set form and is therefore open to suggestion; to being loosely moulded; shaped even. Because of its ease of form it manages to contain things, yet it has great power when necessary, and in the right circumstances and quantity can become a deadly force.

The body is most like water when the fearful mind does not interfere. The looser a falling human body is, the less prone it is to injury. Injuries result because of a certain rigidity adopted as a result of a person's assumption of impact. That is why a person who has no awareness of what is happening to them when they fall (for instance when intoxicated) often end up with fewer injuries than a fully conscious, fretful person.

We often describe people who think in this mode as people who are able to "roll with the punches". We describe them as being "happy-go-lucky" or we identify them as people who don't project their past fears onto present circumstances. They are people who "take life as it comes." Just like the characteristic of water, they learn to contain life in the moment. In general, it is probably the case that most people operate under both mindsets with some being drawn more to one than the other.

Taking the cue from water, I believe that a certain fluidity of consciousness or psychological looseness, if you like, is what is needed to cope with the demands of life. Because you don't know how your choices (or lack of) are going to turn out you might as well cultivate an open and relaxed an attitude towards them as it is possible to have. In so doing, you actually free your mind in order to allow it to create more opportunities. It seems to make sense that in general we shouldn't make that one exam, job or girlfriend the all-important thing in life. We do so at our peril.

However, I am not saying that these things are not important only that it is one thing to put all your energies into obtaining something and another to see it as the only thing worthy of attainment. The one person whom you call Mr or Ms Right may not turn out to be that at all. Like everything else in life, one's own life is far from static and forms part of a continuous process which is constantly evolving and changing. For us, as for water, it seems there are no full stops. On the contrary, life events are all part of one flowing sentence.

An important point to note is that, looking for the positive benefits in life experiences is not the same as saying that every cloud has a silver lining; in fact far from it. To say that every cloud has a silver lining is to put the power in the cloud which then commits you to waiting passively for it to give up that power. Such a position is disempowering because it means that you are not part of an active process insofar as you are the done-to rather than the doer and therefore at the mercy of events.

The point is not that the "bad" things that happen to you necessarily contain good things or things that are necessarily beneficial to you. Rather, based on your current, but potentially limitless understanding, you can choose what is beneficial to you in the "bad" experience in order to both strengthen and develop yourself and in the process lessen the impact of the "bad". That to me is what one aspect of what wisdom is; elevating the base metal of experience to the gold of usefulness, through the process of reflection.

If you are the type of person that values learning then you can look back on a particular "negative" experience and think, "I learned something," which means the so-called bad experience may not represent such a loss, or a big deal, after all. If, on the other hand, a person who has no such philosophy encounters a whole number of experiences that they don't readily welcome, then such a lack of any philosophy increases the burden or the weight of the "bad" experiences.

Think about the athletes who for years fail to win anything and all of a sudden emerge as winners, because all the time they have been "losing" they have been learning. By strengthening both mental and physical muscle they have been preparing themselves to be winners. A world champion of the calibre of British distance runner Paula Radcliffe is just such a person.

Without such an approach we can become bitter, and bitterness acts like rusty nails that seal in our "negative" experiences in the archives of the mind. Power then is to some extent <u>in us</u> and not just in the situation. It is unwise to justify suffering by saying that a "bad" experience contains "good" as though it were like an oyster that contains a pearl. If this was truly the case then people wouldn't end up embittered by their experiences.

I am firmly of the view that you can lessen the burden of an experience in proportion to the use you can make of it. Perhaps this is one reason why people who suffer in particular areas of life are often attracted towards organizations that deal with those areas, and through those organizations they are able to use their experiences to help others. Sometimes where no organization exists they form their own. So, ex-cult members help rescue people from cults. Former gang members that once cut people down without any feelings for their victims now project all their energy into ensuring that other youngsters don't tread the same path.

A useful exercise which I recommend is the following: Choose an experience from the past which you currently label as negative and see if you can draw out any useful experiences from it. For instance, it could be a relationship that went wrong that, although you try to tuck away in the corner of your mind, continually returns to haunt you. You might find that although the experience was painful you have learned something of value that either has or could help you.

Out of such an exercise can come much healing. It's like rescuing land from the sea which gives you a bigger psychological land-base from which to operate. Additionally, such an exercise provides a good basis for getting the practice for thinking in the water consciousness mode. Here are some questions that can help with this task:

- Did I benefit from the experience in any way?

- Did I learn anything about myself?
- Did better opportunities come my way as a result of a certain missed opportunity?
- Did I gain any insight of any kind? Insights can be worth their weight in gold.
- Did I learn any lessons that I was then able to share with others and use to guide them?
- Did I develop my empathy with others as a result?

Because we are creatures of habit, the more we can train ourselves to think in the above way the more it enables this way of thinking to become automatic. Within minutes of a disappointment occurring, you can develop the capacity for exploring the potential it offers for going in a new and fruitful direction.

It all begins with questions. Questions destroy assumptions which are a key feature of Stick Consciousness. Assumptions can only be static as opposed to dynamic and alive. Before you run away from that challenge you should ask yourself whether there is anything that it can teach you. Is there anything that you can use of the experience even if you don't achieve what you set out to achieve?

This is how the two consciousnesses or mindsets, Stick and Water, might declare themselves in response to the following situation:

A Public Speaking Engagement

Stick Consciousness

- I must be able to guarantee perfection otherwise I won't bring myself to do it.
- It must be perfect otherwise it will be a disaster for me.
- Because I cannot guarantee that it will be a great performance, then I will not try it.

- If I fail I will never be able to show myself in public again.
- If I fail I will never attempt such a thing again.

Water Consciousness

- I feel nervous but what are the benefits of undertaking this engagement, regardless of whether or not I achieve an effective performance?
- I will be able to say that I have added to myself.
- I will have challenged myself and challenges make life interesting.
- I will be able to find out what my strengths and weaknesses are in relation to public speaking.
- I might even find that I enjoy the experience which will enable me to give it another try.
- I will have gained knowledge that I can use myself or pass on to others.
- In attempting something I fear, regardless of whether the outcome is successful, I will have demonstrated that I have courage and determination.
- There is a buzz to be gained from taking up a challenge. Challenges are what helps to keep us motivated, happy and on our toes.

In summary, you can gain, potentially, from areas that might be thought of as challenging or even problematic. That this is the case, means that you can project this psychological truth or underpinning of material reality onto any situation that you might have to face in the future. This, in turn should enable you to face it with greater confidence, strength and wisdom. Just being able to do this is a valuable ability in and of itself. It is the same for the novice athlete who knows that although she might not win the next race will look forward to it, with confidence, because what she will learn will help her to move a step closer towards becoming a greater athlete. If further proof is needed about the benefits of converting problems into challenges then consider the reflections on challenge of Dr. Stephen Fuller. Dr. Fuller carried out research into the health giving properties of the herb Ginseng, and has gained vital information on the workings of mind and body. In his book *Ginseng* he notes that:

> Scientists know how challenge wakes up the mind. It does so initially through the production of adrenaline. At the same time, the stress hormones, called corticosteroids… are released by the adrenal glands, travel to the brain and produce motivation, alertness and a readiness to act just as they travel to the muscles and alert them too.[1]

> According to Fuller challenges are even responsible for producing a feeling of well-being.

If you look around you, you can find examples of people who have used their adverse circumstances to benefit them. For instance, Tony Adams, the ex-Arsenal and England footballer, quite admirably attributed the fact that he managed to regain the captaincy of the England team (in the late 90s) and his transformation to a much more rounded and interesting human being, to his determination to overcome his problems with alcohol.

It does not matter whether a person develops their repair-kit philosophy after the ideological vehicle that they have been using to transport them through life has ended up with a flat tyre. The only point worthy of note is that they have found a way of securing a victory out of their adversity. [2]

However, from a Mental Muscle point of view, a more secure position would be to teach yourself to think this way before the occurrence of a crisis that forces such thinking. It is not everyday you fall into a lake and find that your lack of swimming ability is a distinct disadvantage. At such moments you would wish you could swim. To the trained swimmer this presents no such problem of course.

If we were to transpose that example and make it analogous to the things that can go wrong in everyday life to our dreams, plans, wishes and ambitions then we face greater risks of falling into a "Sea of troubles."

Contradictions

There is another related phenomenon that is also potentially very helpful in developing fluidity of consciousness, and that is the contradictions that sometimes exist within situations etc. The word stems from the Latin "contra" meaning against or opposite. We readily meet contradictions when, for instance, one thing we acquire may contain elements or facets of something that we don't want; something that resists, challenges us or stands in opposition to what we do want.

Contradictions are potentially everywhere. You yearn to be married whilst recognizing that it compromises your freedom. You pursue your freedom instead but you end up feeling alone. You might win the lottery and gain all the riches you have ever dreamt of, but end up lonely and dejected because you move out of your circle of friends and your community. You want to live in the country in order to avoid the hustle and bustle of the city, but bemoan the isolation and the lack of excitement in country life. You seek to acquire material things to aide your peace of mind and well-being, but spend all our time worrying about them in case they break or get stolen. On the other hand you sustain an injury, but you meet your future wife in the hospital where you go for treatment. Such a thing happened to Paul Robeson the great singer and actor.

These are the contradictions which can extract a cost with every gain or give something with every loss. The awe-inspiring zenith of the mountain also signals the depth of the drop. The threat of misery resides side by side with the promise of joy. Often our success, in matters of life, depends on resolving the contradictions usually by shifting perspective, as in the statement, "I'd rather be married and my freedom wasn't that fulfilling anyway," or, "Being married cancels out any other benefits that being on my own could bring." By learning to live with and exploit the contradictions we can help to maintain ourselves in peaceful equilibrium.

Contradictions even exist within us with regard to certain qualities and character traits we possess. In certain circumstances qualities we possess can make for a good or bad outcome depending on the context. Think about how close courage is to being reckless and foolhardy; a trait that could wreck a peace deal. A refusal to be easily pushed around, generally, in a negotiation situation could quickly turn to intransigence and mule-like stubbornness. If you shift cowardice along a few degrees it can become a very useful cautiousness. Vanity can be refashioned into a healthy pride. Our weaknesses can become our strengths and our strengths our weaknesses as a Tai Chi teacher once told me.

The martial arts have often exploited this dual feature of human physical and mental ways of being to good effect. Some of the most effective of these arts are the ones that specialise in using an opponent's mental and or physical strengths against them, so that the opponents strength actually becomes a weakness. For instance, an opponent's mental overconfidence might be exploited because the opponent fails to see the weakness in his or her own defence. With regard to the physical side of things, a person's huge height and weight advantage can be used to good effect when they are caught slightly off-balance.

The better martial arts, still, are the ones that teach people how to shift their perspective so that they can see great strength in walking away from a fight, despite the fact that others who look on may think that they are weak.

We, as people, have a variety of methods for dealing with life's contradictions in order to try to maintain our internal harmony. These can run the range from, lying to ourselves as in telling ourselves that there aren't any problems, denial as in refusing to see the extent of a problem, by shifting perspective or by trying to use the problem or incorporate it to our advantage.

As far as I'm concerned the ideal mindset is the latter. It can be represented in an athlete, for instance, who instead of denying the fact that he hates getting up to run would rather face up to this challenge and use it as part of training his mental resolve. He has incorporated the problem to his advantage.

The former athlete Sara Simeoni became the most successful high jumper in history, winning many world titles as well as breaking world records. However, she wanted, initially, to become a dancer, but she was sent packing from ballet school because she was thought of as being too tall. She didn't become ground down by the experience and lost in regret. Like the element water, when faced with an obstacle, she merely took a diversion around her blocked path. She learned a different form of flight to the balletic kind by becoming a high jumper.

The mental muscle programme is not about denying or distorting what is, for the sake of an uneasy internal peace but about facing up to what is for a higher gain. You can change perspective by asking how the contradiction can be put to some use, or can be of benefit. People can and do shift perspectives when it suits them and they can even find a way of embracing things that work against them by doing so. This is most important from the point of view of converting something from a problem to a challenge and, further down the line, even to an opportunity. This is a theme I shall expand upon in the next chapter.

The notion of the usefulness of contradictions has found no better symbolic expression, in my opinion, than in the ancient Yin, Yang symbol (Figure 1 on the following pages). Originating in ancient China the symbol manages to express a unity amongst opposites. You have a circle cut into two equal portions with black on one side and white on the other which represent the forces of opposition. Yet they are contained within a circle.

At the most basic level the outer circle represents harmony and unity when opposites are held in balance. So night needs day, up accompanies down, sorrow is matched with joy and hatred allows the possibility of love. If that wasn't enough, both the white portion and the black contain smaller circles with their opposite colour. This suggests that each contain elements of the other; a feature which is also important for harmony. For instance, in loving (positive), it might be right that we express a little anger (negative) in order to convey some concern for a loved one who is engaged in some kind of foolhardy action.

The small circles could even represent the idea that there is a little "bad" in the best of us and a little "good" in the worst of us.

The symbol, as a whole, can be used to apply to character and the need for certain elements in order to keep the character balanced. Imagine, for instance, a person who is very timid; a quality represented by one of the shaded portions of the circle. If this person is timid to the point of ending up a victim then it can only do some good to introduce just a hint of the opposite of timidity, perhaps represented by the small circle, just as you would introduce an essence of some juice to water in order to flavour it. This is very useful, particularly in cultures that don't readily celebrate or value the shy, the passive and the introverted.

Another example, from an alternative health point of view, is Homeopathy. The art of the Homeopath is to take a diseased body and put it at its ease but it does this by introducing a little element of the disease (the opposite) in order to encourage the body to fight back.

Finally, the symbol hints at the need for resistance; for things to move against us in order that we can develop holistically. Just think about what our bodies would be like without gravity as a form or resistance? The lack of gravity in space is one reason why astronauts have to exercise in space, otherwise they would lose bone density.

Figure 1. Yin Yang symbol

Contradictions, then, can be of use to you. When something goes wrong in the choices you make you can exploit the contradictions in order that you can lessen the potentially wounding nature of the experience. The fact that an experience can change from being something of a nuisance to something of a use is central, indeed the foundation of what this mental muscle programme is about.

The threat of death and crisis also helps us to shift perspective. Sometimes it is that one little bit of crisis that teaches us to see things from a new perspective. Would you really be worrying about that new car if you knew that the world was going to end tomorrow? You have to imagine that some people would dream of having some of the problems you have in exchange for a moment more of life whilst they face the prospect of a terminal disease.

On the other hand, sometimes, we never feel more alive than when we are faced by a crisis. Somehow it focuses us and forces us to envelop the moment. The now-deceased writer Dennis Potter, who knew he had only months to live, when asked in an interview about how his condition affected his life once said, "Never did blossom seem blossomier." For Potter his condition heightened both the preciousness and the value of life. It helped him to see and feel more of life; perhaps see and feel things that it might take some of us five lifetimes to be able to see and feel.[3]

I remember as a child being fascinated by the tightly wound metal bands in clocks that formed the basis of a clock's ability to keep the time. I was captivated by the condensed energy and power in the wound up band, and how that power wasn't the same once I unravelled the band. For Dennis Potter, it seems, the experience he underwent concentrated life's vitality into a shorter time space.

One area where it is often expected that people will always experience only loss, and no benefit, is in areas such as that of disfigurement. However, even in this area it cannot be taken for granted that there isn't any gain. This is not to say that there is no pain involved in certain conditions. I am merely trying to comment on the fact that the human spirit, when it has to, has a great capacity for being able to extract something positive from many situations.

In *Overcoming Disfigurement,* Doreen Trust relates the story of a man who, from his viewpoint, suffered so much pain and isolation as a result of his disfigurement, that he decided to undergo a series of cosmetic operations in order to "correct" his condition. Was he happy with the result? He had this to say:

"I ventured into the world only to find something was missing. Why do people no longer look at me? What do I have to do to attract attention? A sense of discontent came over me." [4]

Now I am not saying that life doesn't deal people a bad hand. Rather, I want to illustrate how the quoted example demonstrates two main things. The first is how people have the ability to shift their perspective on things. The second, is how something positive, such as an appreciation of life, can be bravely extracted from a "tragic" situation. Where changing a situation isn't a viable alternative then using it, if you can, surely is.

Whatever the challenge is, consciousness, like a great magician, has the capacity to make your limitations, whatever they might be; less a ceiling blocking your ascent, and more of an open sky towards which you can soar.

The implications for us

What I want you to try to digest from this chapter is that, given that "bad' things can transform into "good", you might as well have as positive an attitude to all the challenges that come your way as it is possible to have. It is the basis for helping you dare to try; particularly, to dare to tackle the things you might shy away from tackling. It is a foundation upon which you can decide to make your goals realisable and look forward to taking on the challenges that can that stand between you and the manifestation of those goals.

Similarly, the runner who, emerges to win the race, didn't emerge fully formed. She started from somewhere, somewhere that may have been quite a small beginning, and then built on this foundation. Perhaps she started with just daring to try.

Chapter 2

The Basics Of Mental Muscle

"Don't run from what hurts you. Sometimes what hurts you is all you've got. Learn to use what hurts you."

James Baldwin: Amen Corner.

The mind, that essential part of ourselves which collects information, filters and processes our experiences (amongst other things known and unknown) acts in similar fashion to a muscle. And, although natural development, especially during the adolescent phase, does account for some growth, all muscles develop, mostly, through the overcoming of resistance. Anything that resists the body in some way is capable of building muscle and that resistance can take on various forms. All of the following constitute resistance:

- Lifting a heavy object;
- Using all or parts of the body to push against a static object such as a wall;
- Movement through anything heavier than air; swimming being the perfect example;
- Holding up parts of the body such as an arm or leg for extended periods of time.

One of the reasons why it is worthwhile mentioning the various forms or resistance that affect the body, is that I want you to realise that this is analogous to the myriad of ways that the mind can be resisted and therefore enabled to build up mental muscle.

On a physical level, through the systematic and sustained use of resistance – the best method for building up muscle – the tissues in the body are broken down and are reconstituted in a stronger manner. The addition of a good diet will facilitate the best gains in muscular development. Just as we know that muscles develop and grow by adapting to the workload, i.e., the next time round being able to lift more or stretch further, so too does mental muscle have its indicators of growth. What do I mean by mental muscular growth?

Mental muscular growth, unlike with anatomical muscle cannot, by and large, be measured by physical means. It is invisible. The only yardstick of its existence is a change in behaviour or attitude; a demonstration of learning and/or a development of the finer psychological elements or traits, such as understanding, sensitivity, courage, love and empathy. We may not be able to measure these areas of mental growth but we certainly acknowledge and respond to their presence.

Mental muscular growth or development appears in many incarnations. One form in which it appears is when people accommodate to circumstances that present some degree of difficulty, such as a move to a new neighbourhood.

Here is one example of adaptation taken from the sports world, related in the book *Sporting Body, Sporting Mind* by John Syer and Christopher Connolly. At the height of the cold war, Russian athletes were unpopular in Western countries. In order to get them to accommodate to strongly hostile crowds their coaches took to organising practice sessions on home territory where the sound of a "jeering crowd was played out on loudspeakers. The players became "used to it." They learnt to adapt so that when faced with the real thing their performances would not be adversely affected. [1]

We talk in terms of people being able to adjust. We even recognize the fact that people can accommodate to their experience of an institution to such an extent that it makes it difficult for them to cope or adjust to new circumstances.

We call this being institutionalised. This phenomenon has been widely observed in people such as prisoners who have been incarcerated for long periods of time. Perhaps this is the mental equivalent of being physiologically muscle-bound: a body strengthened in such a one-dimensional way that it becomes less suited to a variety of tasks and physical challenges.

It maybe in the area of what psychologists refer to as *Habituation* where mental muscular growth is most clearly demonstrated. This is an important concept for us to grasp. Psychologists Atkinson, Atkinson and Hilgard, in *The Introduction to Psychology,* define habituation as "The reduction in the strength of a response to a repeated stimulus." A stimulus is simply any event, thing, or incident that either excites or causes a state of arousal in a living organism. If you've ever had a noisy party going on next door whilst you've been trying to sleep then you certainly know what a stimulus is. Additionally, a stimulus can be internal or external.[2]

The word habituation, simply put, means you get used to a stimulus or something that arouses through constant exposure. In turn, the degree of response it provokes in you can diminish. People who move from the quiet of the country into the non-stop noise-carnival of city life adjust by way of tuning out the excess as a result of constant exposure. You can tune out the sound of the ticking clock or the dawn chorus.

The reverse is also true, of course, which is the point at which we talk about people becoming sensitized. The dripping tap can seem like the noisiest thing in the world to a vulnerable person: to someone with a weakened mental muscle in other words. The understanding of these mechanisms has come to form the basis of psychological behaviour modification techniques that can be applied to solving such problems as fears and phobias. Consequently, progressive and systematic exposure to a fear-provoking animal such as a snake is a proven means of ridding a person of their phobia. This is known as Behavioural Therapy.

A stimulus can appear in many forms. It could start out life as your own anxious state or somebody else's. It could appear as something you have to face up to or a task to be completed. In whatever way a stimulus manifests, it can act as a challenge to you. The most important point is that it can be adapted to, incorporated, or simply just overcome.

Elaine Aron makes this clear in her brilliant book about sensitive people called *The Highly Sensitive Person*. She states that:

> It is often the case that the more your body acts-looks out of the window, goes bowling, travels, speaks in public- the less difficult and arousing it becomes. This is called habituation. If it is a skill, you also become better at it. For example, travelling alone in a foreign country can seem utterly overwhelming to a HSP [highly sensitive person]. And you may always choose to avoid some aspect of it. But the more you do it, the easier it becomes....[3]

As far as the development of mental muscle is concerned, getting better at something is just another way of saying that the mental muscle became strengthened. Mental muscular growth is demonstrated in other ways. You grow mentally insofar as you gain wisdom and knowledge, particularly if you are able to learn and reflect on lessons from significant experiences. You improve and grow stronger, particularly, if you take on challenges systematically.

For example, you decide that you would like to take part in a play; your very first performance. As it's your first time you may be over-anxious which produces either a below par or stilted performance.

However, if you decide to persevere with this interest; reflect on your mistakes and project what you have learned onto your next venture then you should have grown. You might learn that one way forward may be to try and enjoy the experience; to focus on the audience instead of your anxiety or even to develop a devil-may-care, it's-not-the-end-of-the-world attitude. You might even learn to work more efficiently, comfortably and with less effort.

One of the most essential indicators of the presence of growth is that you should be able to do more in particular areas. Just as physiological muscular growth allows you to lift more weight, so should you be able to take on more of the same challenge or more of other challenges.

These types of mental gains or growth have their recognition in everyday and commonplace sayings such as, "You get used to it," "You learn by your experiences" or by your "mistakes" or even, "Nothing ventured nothing gained."

Problems, as I have already outlined in the last chapter, are nothing but a form of resistance; an obstacle that blocks your path which you must develop mental muscle in order to shift. What do these obstacles resist? Well for a start your will, your desires, your needs, your urges and your emotional hunger for satisfaction and peace amongst others.

But you know that that which resists can cause growth, mental muscular growth. You know from the discussions in the last chapter that resistance, if seen as a challenge rather than a problem, can both benefit as well as enrich you. The real question is not whether you can turn something to your benefit but how much of it can you benefit from?

What is quite significant and of interest to this programme is the degree to which people in this culture look upon facing challenges as a weight-bearing activity. We talk of suffering under the yoke, millstones around our necks, and people on our backs, of overload, buckling under the strain, the weight of expectation, heavy situations, and carrying a heavy load etc. Consider the following phrases which seem to reinforce this observation:

- "We all have our crosses to bear."
- "She's weighed down by it all."
- "He's carrying the whole world on his shoulders."
- "Too much for such young shoulders to carry."
- "It's more than I can bear."
- "I feel as though everything's on top of me."
- "You're bringing along too much emotional baggage."

The purpose of making such intuitive recognition explicit is to demonstrate not only that we already have an image for life's challenges, but in mental muscle we also have a metaphor for framing an understanding of growth.

The starting line up. Putting on the training shoes

The more accustomed name for resistance and challenges are problems (depending on our outlook of course). This is particularly the case when we are in the mode of consciousness (namely stick). This mode wants to concern itself with only that which it is focused on without any by-products, by way of difficulties.

"Problem" is a term that is more usually associated with the negative and insurmountable. It tends to denote an obstacle that will break your back to shift; something that you should shout and scream at for spoiling the fun; something that you, essentially, should run away from.

All words have associations which have been built up over time. Consequently, they have power through those associations to cause certain effects in our minds.

By either re-examining particular words or substituting them, you can renegotiate the relationship you have with them and their powerful associations. So, as in keeping with the lessons of the previous chapter – that you never know how things are going to turn out; instead of thinking of the resistance to your will as a problem, the first step, or task, as far as this programme is concerned, is to see it as a challenge.

I am not saying that it will be easy to do this with all situations. The mind takes time to accommodate to and assimilate new thinking. It needs sustained training and practice in order to embrace the new, so that the new can become internalised, and therefore become second nature. That is why so much of our learning is based on repetition. That applies to the things we learn for both the body and the mind.

But let us see this as the beginning of the training; the first point or the putting on of the training shoes if you like. The act of putting on the shoes for the person not used to the training can be a positive act. It can be seen as a bold declaration: an act of saying, "Yes", an acknowledgement or symbol of the willingness not only to make the best out of a situation but to get something positive out of it.

Before adopting this way of thinking just pause for a moment and think about the major psychological significance of this shift in perspective. What should be realised is that the word "challenge" unlike, the word "problem", suggests that you *can* get something out of it. Deep down we all like a challenge and, I believe, as I shall go on to outline, that we wither through the lack of them. That metaphorical rock in the path may be of benefit to us; just as (literally speaking) a rock in the path of the willing runner is a welcome tool for increasing stamina and strength etc. By providing something she has to jump over the rock offers the benefit of exercising more muscle.

Such a perspective, concerning the nature of "the challenge," allows different types of questions to loom in the mind such as, "How can I use this situation to benefit me?" rather than, "How is this going to stop my plans from coming to fruition?" A question such as that of the former is the beginning of empowerment because it converts your position from being less of a done-to to more of a doer.

By way of analogy, the point I am trying to make is this: to a person who isn't an athlete, who lives a sedentary life, a hill presents a problem; an obstacle to their desire to tread the easy route home. To the athlete training for accomplishment it is a Godsend because of the more pronounced resistance it offers. The only real difference between the two people is that the latter sees something of benefit to the hill.

Thinking about challenges is no different. It rather reminds me of certain people who in reference to life say "I prefer to think of the glass as half full rather than half empty." Whether the glass is seen as half full or half empty generates different sorts of psychological consequences. The latter perspective has the potential to lead to despair and a focus on loss, and the former has the potential to lead to peace, inner fulfilment and enrichment.

If you can perceive resistance, effectively, as a challenge rather than as a problem, in your mind, you are effectively converting the energy contained within that resistance from abuse energy – energy that will terrorise your psyche – into use-energy or energy that will benefit you. That is why it is always advantageous to turn whatever resists you into something useful.

This may be one of the principle reasons why a variety of people respond to the same stressful situation differently, with the stressful situation taking more or less different tolls according to the persons philosophical outlook, training, personality, motivation, reason for being in the situation, expectation of outcome, as well as the interpretation they give to the event.

All will have some sort of bearing on whether a situation is deemed more or less stressful. I am not trying to argue that stress is something that merely exists inside our own heads. There are situations that are widely recognized as undoubtedly creating more stress than others such as moving house, changing jobs and coping with loss. All I am simply presenting is the case that different people respond to stress differently and the effects of a stressful situation can be modified.

Perhaps a similar thing can be said of the response to pain. A boxer might suffer a broken nose but may not register the pain in the heat of battle; the motivation and expected glory, as well as the adrenaline, having some bearing on the degree to which the pain is registered. But imagine the same person reclining in a bar and a stranger comes and thumps him. It is possible that the perceived injustice would add to the pain. In both scenarios the key element is the degree of control a person has over the situation which renders it either innocuous or not.

Ronald Melzack writing in the *Puzzle of Pain* has this to say about the part that our interpretation and what we bring to a situation, etc, plays in the registration and perception of pain:

> In higher species at least, there is much evidence that pain is not simply a function of the amount of bodily damage alone. Rather, the amount and quality of pain we feel are also determined by our previous experiences and how well we remember them, by our ability to understand the cause of the pain and to grasp its consequences. Even the culture in which we have been brought up plays an essential part in how we feel and respond to pain.

So pain itself is mediated by all types of psychological and cultural influences and interventions. Melzack adds: "Pain perception, then, cannot be defined simply in terms of particular kinds of stimuli. Rather it is a highly personal experience, depending on cultural learning, the meaning of the situation, and other factors that are unique to each individual." [4]

Once again I would not argue that there aren't any painful events external to us: that would be nonsense. But there is a lot to be said for the part played by our own mind's interpretation. This can be further demonstrated by the phenomena known as "phantom limbs". This relates to situations where people who have had amputations to limbs have, on occasion, for reasons that are still not fully understood, given accounts of being in severe pain in a region in space that a limb used to occupy. Despite having a foot missing they may complain of pain in the absent foot, hence the term phantom limb. This goes some way towards demonstrating that the mind plays a major part in deeming what is painful. [5]

There is also an interesting phenomenon involving parents and young children that may shed further light on how interpretation plays a part in pain. A child, when he or she falls, will often look to the significant adult, in a moment of stillness as if wanting them to interpret the severity of the event for them. Some adults deliberately choose to treat the fall lightly as if not to set too low a limit for a response for the child. This suggests that the adult world may play some part in scaffolding a child's interpretation of what it deems as painful for relatively low-key incidents. Adults teach children how to interpret the world, as well as the fact that children teach themselves through experience.

This understanding is helpful in terms of building the confidence to wilfully and deliberately meet the challenges that are so much a part of life. If you can meet these challenges then you can lessen the pain of them.

On the whole, you should take a positive stance towards the situations and events that you have to face up to and would like to do so with less duress, particularly if there is no other alternative. At the time of writing, I am tempted to bemoan the lack of work that has come my way from the teaching agency I work for.

On the other hand, from a mental muscle perspective, this situation allows me the opportunity to write this piece which is my goal. What really matters is that the philosophy has given me peace of mind and enables me to keep down the stress I could be feeling. At the very least I am helping myself by committing to paper what I feared committing to paper, thus proving to myself that I can do it.

However, it has given me more than that. It has given me immense enthusiasm which I have reinvested back into other aspects of life. Sometimes whilst writing, the inspiration I have felt has been incredible; often a real high. So you can see with that slight shift in perspective I have allowed myself not only to see how I have benefited on a number of different levels but also to have reaped the energy of those benefits.

Like the athlete who still focuses on winning that shiny trophy, or passing the line first, as the case may be, I still maintain my goal of having my work published. But I am not going to miss all the many benefits I have gained along the way, which in some respect may be better than attaining the actual goal.

An athlete who is goal-focused only is half an athlete because they are half a person. It will be hard to motivate such a person if they are not motivated by the prize. Someone who is enthusiastic about all aspects of the athletic life and is able to appreciate the many ways that they benefit from it, can use their enthusiasm as a stepping stone for reaching the goal. The goal might be the destination but the recognition of the benefits is the fuel for powering the way there.

Sometimes the athlete, for whom winning is everything, misses out on appreciating the by-products that being involved in athletics has given them such as, increased physical health and an enhanced self-esteem . Winning becomes so paramount, some will even cheat to get to the finishing line first, or jump further than anyone else. We too can become so blinded by our attempts at success that we miss out on the beneficial by-products of our endeavours, a state of being or thinking which can leave our lives so shrunken that we fail to appreciate the good things around us.

To restate the point, stage one of facing any challenge is to ask yourself how you might benefit from the obstacle. In psychologically converting the "problem" from abuse of you to use to you, the load is already being lightened to something more manageable.

I taught this technique to a group of students I was teaching at an evening class. As a prelude to trying to get my students to accept challenges in areas where they felt quite weak, namely speaking out in class, I asked a group of them, who were quite reserved, what it felt like to answer questions in class. I asked them about all the negative emotions that they associated with the task. They said they felt nervous, anxious, fearful and scared that they might make a fool of themselves.

I then asked them what sort of positive things they might feel as a result of speaking out. They said that they would probably feel excitement, pride in themselves for having risen to the challenge, and would recognize that they were courageous. I wanted them to appreciate the fact that although negative emotions could be conjured up by an event, so too could positive ones. I then suggested that they focus on the expected positive emotions as a way of motivating themselves.

After an exercise where one of the students had to talk about her assignment in front of the class, she said that although her nerves held her back, she was so proud of her achievement because, on her terms, she did quite well. This was especially the case given the fact that English was not her first language. Despite the potential negatives, she gained enormously just by conceptualising the "problem" in a different way.

The usefulness of resistance

I would argue that we need resistance or challenges from a mental muscle point of view. Just as the body needs physical resistance, or the muscles atrophy, so too do we need challenges both mental and physical otherwise we atrophy mentally. I would even go on to say that I believe senility may be in part due to a lack of intellectual challenges at a stage in life where it is no longer easy for the mind, at a cellular level, as well as the body, to renew itself – because of age – so this must be done consciously.

The problem with the diminishing of mental muscle can extend to people who suddenly come into possession of great wealth, as in a lottery win. One reason lottery winners come unstuck when they come into possession of vast sums of money is because they don't seem to realise how they systematically built up their mental muscle in order to cope with the struggles of life.

They forget about the little philosophies they develop which keep them moving against the resistance offered by the material world. Some also forget, too, the reinforced support from the community that help to "lift" the challenges; the many hands that help to make light of the work. Many so-called winners abandon, all too quickly, an accustomed way of life and then wonder why they feel lost.

All these elements can come to form an integral part of our mental anatomy. One lottery winner in the 90's came face to face with the implication of his win. He said; "Before I had been aggressive, wanting to win. But I'd lost all that drive; I had nothing to strive for anymore." All of a sudden he had no more use for the muscle he had accumulated, particularly the one concerned with motivation. He was like the athlete who had won it all.[6]

You should not underestimate the importance of the muscle you build up through the life patterns you establish. The sudden liberation from the need for various kinds of social skill can be like the following: Imagine a person who has worked hard on her land for most of her life. In response she has developed a powerful physique which suits the nature of the work. Someone comes along and offers her the use of a robot to take over every single chore she can think of.

What then happens to her physical strength? It simply diminishes. Of course I am not arguing that people shouldn't be spared back-breaking work, only for a balance in the physical and mental sphere which allows for the separation between the necessary and the unnecessary. Nor am I arguing that that people should be without money. I am simply demonstrating the way that mental muscle accumulated over time as a result of trying social circumstances can diminish.

The withering away of the mental muscle can be seen in other areas. For instance, because there is such an overuse of the calculator people are not so adept at doing mental arithmetic. As a teacher I attended a seminar once where a primary school teacher bemoaned the lack of skill, amongst children, in this area. It is interesting to note that as scientists enthuse about computers that can do "this, that and the other" better than humans, potentially relegating us to bystanders on the mega highway of computer progress, we may be in danger of becoming the equivalent of intellectual couch potatoes.

Think about the athlete about to compete for the first time in their first major event. Imagine the nerves involved. Imagine the sick-to-the-stomach feeling that might be enough to make him wish that he had decided on another career, as he faces an enormous crowd that is hungry for action. So overwhelming is the feeling that it is difficult to come to terms with. Then think about the same person when he is in the twilight of his career; when the magic has gone and everything seems so commonplace. Don't you think that he would long for the freshness of that challenge; with all its attendant baggage of fear and excitement? I often think that people fear the commonplace, the banal and the boring as much as they fear anything in life.

This scenario can be transposed into many situations that are new; that first job as a teacher, lawyer or labourer: that first job, full stop. How often do you hear people say, after doing the same thing for a number of years, that no matter how interesting it was originally, "It no longer gives me the excitement it used to." Have you noticed how you now begin to rue the day that you found your job fairly easy after once finding it difficult?

You might have started out thinking: "This is so hard that I'll never be able to master it," only to find that some weeks, months, or years down the line it comes too easy for you and you find yourself hankering for the early days when there was so much resistance offered. This is the mental muscle crying out for a fresh challenge. People, as a matter of course, get used to and accommodate to all types of challenges.

I'll never forget the time, when as a youth, my mother let me got to my first Northern Soul All-nighter; a place called Wigan Casino. Wigan Casino was the Mecca for the devotees of the strangely beautiful, acrobatic dance that still is Northern Soul. People would dance all night to the music which held quite a fascination for its pilgrims.

I'll never forget the mixture of awe and terror I felt as I crossed its threshold and came across something that was much larger than I was. After I got used to the scene I forever hankered after the time when everything was so fresh and challenging that it frightened the life out of me; when a sense of awe was gift-wrapped in anxious anticipation and excitement. Let us not forget that one of the times when we probably feel most alive, and in and of the moment, is when we are being challenged by something. It wakes up all our senses which is the reason why, of course, people often put themselves in controlled danger, through taking up such pursuits as skydiving and mountaineering.

Pre-event training

In my view, one of the keys to facing up to one or a series of challenges such as changing our behaviour patterns, whether it has to do with plucking up courage to speak in a seminar or trying to find the voice to speak our mind to a partner, is to set about planning or making changes outside of the situation that requires such changes.

It is very hard to achieve a goal in a demanding situation (another kind of resistance) for which we are not prepared, especially if we feel that we do not already possess the resources for being able to do so. For example, for someone who is not used to talking to the opposite sex and has no natural confidence, just talking to someone out the blue can be very difficult. If an offer is rejected this can be devastating to the person concerned.

In athletic terms, under normal circumstances, we would not expect a person to decide to run and complete, successfully, a twenty mile marathon, without training. Some people do have a natural stamina or certain resilience that may allow them to undertake such an endeavour, just as some people can be thick-skinned enough to talk to the opposite sex, with a view to dating. However, this is not the same as training for the event. Most of us mere mortals need training to accomplish that which we are not used to trying to accomplish or which may be slightly beyond either our expectations of ourselves or what we can presently cope with.

We quite willingly accept this fact when training to acquire a specific skill, like that of becoming a computer engineer or a teacher, but when it comes to issues such as that of changing behaviour patterns we are not so accepting. Why? It is probably because we don't have a concept of being able to do so. We have not been so trained to look at aspects of our psychological life in this way. At school we are not taught how to train the mind for its own sake or for the purpose of enabling us to cope well with life. Rather, the emphasis on training is placed, mostly, on shaping people to fit the needs of the economy and whatever demands it happens to make. Therefore, it treats people as a means to an end, by and large.

The bulk of the work for making changes is best done outside of the situation or point where a desired action is called for. The idea is to train for the moment or the event so to speak, just like a hurdler would train intensively outside of his event or specific moment of challenge. Armed with this understanding, this is what you are laying the foundation for. Let us now look at the specific mindset that needs to be developed in order to create the impetus for facing challenges with confidence.

The "I can do it" mindset

In order to confront a situation, one that offers resistance, in the form of anxiety, fear, apprehension, then it helps if you can create a positive attitude towards the task; preferably in the form of what I like to call the "I can do it", attitude. Far from this mindset being just an arrogant position suggesting that you are going to succeed no matter what, without putting any effort into what you are called to do, it is much more than that. It is about creating a favourable mindset that can provide the basis for building the self belief that will enable you to achieve your aims.

Supposing a person wants to run and complete a marathon, it helps her to believe she can do it if she can draw upon a similar experience of achievement in her past. For instance she might say to herself, "I once ran five miles to get to the nearest garage because my car had broken down, and although it was an exceptional circumstance that prompted my action, it taught me that not only did I not drop dead from exhaustion, but I am not that unfit. I would like to try to run a marathon."

That experience becomes part of a frame of reference which can support the positive mindset that she now wants to cultivate, with respect to running the marathon; namely, the "I can do it", mindset. This attitude is important. As long as a person is saying "I can" then they are opening up the door to positive mental forces.

A fascinating aspect of human psychology is that positive and negative results come hard on the back of positive and negative attitudes respectively. That is why athletes, no matter how off-peak or unconfident they might be feeling, never – insofar as they can help it – think in terms of not being able to achieve their goal; that of winning. They know that such thinking will only inhibit their performance. Just look at the mental preparations boxers undertake before a fight and at the pre-match conference. Neither party will express the view that they think they are going to lose. For our potential marathon runner who has no such experience to draw on the positive mindset has to be built up.

In terms of making changes to your life, generally speaking you are probably in a better position than the novice athlete. Look back over your personal development and you will find that you can always find some experience in your life that can help you to achieve some goal or other that you have, whether that goal has to do with changing an aspect of behaviour or carrying out a challenging task that is foreign to you.

These experiences can and should be used to provide a foundation for supporting your goal. For instance, let's consider the person who has a vague notion that they would like to try their hand at teaching. That person might think, initially, that the challenge of becoming a teacher is far beyond any experience that they have had in their life, therefore, they have no foundation on which to build themselves up for the task.

However, if they look imaginatively at their experiences they might see a lot that can be used to support the task. They might have spoken up at a public meeting or two, and may realise that this is not a world away from teaching. If they have children, then as a parent they are also first stage teachers. All these things can be drawn upon in order to build the "I can do it" attitude. I must stress that the creation of this positive mindset is not to replace the work towards ones task. Preparation must still be done.

With a little bit of thought a wide range of qualities can be used to support you in a task. Perhaps you can draw on a dogged determination that you know you possess or even a stubbornness that you have displayed at times. With a little bit of imagination quite a lot of your experiences, attitudes, habits and idiosyncrasies, can be recycled in order to aid you in certain situations.

Exercise

With this in mind, I think that it would be a good idea to make a list of the qualities that you have, so that you can appreciate, quite clearly, the mental and emotional resources that you can bring towards achieving your future goals. Be generous to yourself when doing this, and do try to push beyond the bounds that you normally think within, especially if you suffer from low self-esteem.

Just as the potential athlete is subjected to a lot of testing so that she can be given the right sort of training programme for development, as well as to enable her to be suited to the right type of sport, it is good for you to know your qualities so that you can draw on them when you need them. They can then be tailored to suit certain situations.

A good athlete knows what she is capable of. She will know how her muscles work; how best to feed them; how they recover, as well as what loads they can carry. For the novice athlete it is critical that they are assessed in order to meet the demands of training, to find out how fast they can go; how far they can go, or just how much they can carry.

From the mental athlete's point of view you also need to document your mental capabilities so that you can find the appropriate challenges for the mental levels at which you operate.

It is for this reason that I believe we should exercise great caution when giving people advice in an, if-I-were-you-I-would-do-this, kind of way. Often people offer advice too much from their own capabilities rather than trying to offer what might be consistent with the person's own level, potential and capabilities. Some of us, other than when our lives are in danger, are not always ready to cope with the consequences of actions dictated by others which might be beyond our capabilities.

Additionally, when completing the list see how many qualities can be used for any immediate situations or challenges that you may have to face. Such an exercise enables you to bring to consciousness that which you have; fully usable resources so that they don't end up like the type of forgotten goods you keep in a pantry; full of dust and neglected to the point where you don't know how to make use of them. Knowing what you are capable of is so essential to building confidence. It is called knowing yourself. It is something that quite a number of spiritual traditions placed a lot of emphasis on.

Chapter 3

Weights For The Mind

"Every crisis, no matter how upsetting at first, brings an opportunity to grow in positive ways"

Wendy Malz: The Sexual Healing Journey.

If a "weight," used for building up the body, is just another variation on the theme of resistance then we know that this resistance can be found everywhere. For those of us who want to build up the body we don't necessarily need nicely sculpted weights in a soft-carpeted gym in order to achieve this ambition. If you can't afford the membership fee for the local gym why sit idle? Why not use bricks housed safely in a rucksack.

Think of the person who is desperate to become an athlete but who lacks resources. That shopping they have to carry would become a tool for their physiological development as would the timber to be chopped. "Why take the car, when you can shape your legs for free, by walking?" they would reason. You can use the body as a form of resistance or a weight by way of push ups. You can even get a rope and use parts of the body to pull against it. It is all resistance. Simply put, we can use what is to hand to train ourselves.

You can develop a similar approach of using what is to hand, during the course of everyday life, in order to develop yourself mentally. The weights for the mind can be found everywhere both internally and externally and in many forms. Let's look at internal resistance for a moment. At its simplest, when one part of you works against, contradicts or frustrates another part of you, then this is resistance. If you want internal peace and you have anxiety instead then the anxiety constitutes resistance, because the anxiety works against your desire for peace.

Worry is another form of resistance. So is fear, particularly when it is not connected to anything which currently exists in the external environment. Struggling with doubt or thoughts that you will never be good at anything is resistance. Any negative habit of thought that you desire to change, by so doing setting yourself up in opposition to it, is resistance and is therefore a weight for the mind.

On occasion you might find it hard to let go of some irritation that bugs you for no discernable reason. You try and tell yourself to let it go; to forget it. At the moment when you challenge the irritation and it doesn't leave you then you have resistance. All these elements can also be attached to external situations giving you a dual resistance to cope with. Worry, for instance, might be attached to a real concern about losing your job. On the other hand, the irritation you feel might stem from a wounding comment a person has made.

As for the external weights for the mind, these also exist everywhere in a variety of forms: the car alarm sounding when you are trying to get some sleep; the frustration caused by not fulfilling your dreams; the salesperson that rips you off; the lack of money that you possess or the injury that you have sustained that must be overcome. The relationship that eludes you is at one and the same time an aspect of resistance. These are all weights for the mind.

I hope it is now clear that you have resistance that you are confronted by everyday that is the mind's equivalent of lifting a weight. But what you also need to appreciate, from the point of view of this programme, is that these weights are not all of the same value.

They run the range from light to heavy and therefore exert different demands upon the mind just as real weights do upon the body. That is to say that events ranging from minor irritations to major upsets seek to work against us and extract a different toll on our resources. Therefore, you need to try to make a mental note of their weighting or the degree to which they present difficulties so that at least you can develop appropriate forms of action for dealing with them or making use of them.

In the minor irritation category (the light weight) might be a person who sits next to you and starts smoking. In the same category, or lower down the scale, might be the fact that you are stuck in a queue in the supermarket; a situation that is complicated further by the fact that you are tired and haven't eaten all day.

Sometimes there is not a lot we can do with these events. They are foisted on us by life in all its interesting manifestations, so we might as well try to use them to benefit us by taking the mental muscle approach.

However, what qualifies as a major or minor irritation also depends on your present psychological make up. The degree to which some forms of resistance are seen as light, or heavy, vary between individuals to some extent.

No two people are exactly the same. We all have our different strengths, weaknesses and tolerances. There may be things that wind us up universally but the point at which we react can vary from person to person. This is why, once again, it is worthwhile getting to know yourself very well and why I asked you to complete the exercises at the end of the last chapter. This is not dissimilar to physical strength. The big oak table that might seem like a heavy weight to one person may feel quite light in the hands of a strong man or woman.

The question of how you can use situations, offering resistance, depends both on what you need and the specific mental muscle you wish to train. As a side note, because we are dealing with mind in all its richness I prefer to split up psychological qualities into separate areas of mental muscle.

When you think about muscle in relation to the body you can think about it in either of two ways. On the one hand you can think about the body as being one large muscular mass enveloping the skeleton. On the other hand you also know that this mass can be broken up into separate areas; muscle groups and sub-groups. For instance, there are the biceps (front of arms); triceps (back of arms) and abdominals (stomach muscles).

The "isolation" of specific muscle groups can be crucial when it comes to working the body. Different muscle groups need to be focused upon and worked differently in order to obtain maximum benefit. Some require specific types of exertion or repetitions of weight-bearing exercises in order to promote growth. For instance, it is common for bodybuilders to perform more repetitions with a weight when working the legs than when working the arms. Individual athletes will concentrate on working specific muscle groups to aid them in the event they specialise in.

The mind, from a mental muscle point of view, has various facets which are subdivisions of its overall capability. Qualities, or facets, such as patience, courage and friendliness etc, I see as individual components of the "mental anatomy", that make a contribution to the mind's overall strength.

So let's go back to the question of what you need and the specific mental muscle you wish to train. You might be an impatient person so the queue presents you with an ideal opportunity to develop the patience muscle. With this in mind you can train yourself by simply waiting patiently and trying to relax both mind and body. At the same time you can be attentive to signs of tension in the body; an indication that you are becoming stressed.

To increase the intensity of the training you could try smiling while you are waiting. To increase the resistance still further (if you are still within a zone of comfort, or finding it surprisingly pleasant to have discovered stillness) you could even let that nice man behind you, who has just happened to come out in his slippers, go in front of you. If you are keen or perhaps slightly generous you can even let the whole queue in front of you.

By carrying out actions such as these you relay a symbolic message back to yourself that some aspects of life simply aren't worth rushing around for. When you rush around you can miss all the humorous, the generous and the interesting things along the way. And, let's not forget about the benefits to be had from developing internal stillness as opposed to being stimulated by a state of anxiety?

Let us return to the question of the person who is smoking beside you. There could be various scenarios which could all offer differing levels of resistance.

Scenario 1: people are allowed to smoke and there aren't any other seats available to move to. Scenario 2: there is a no smoking sign which the person who is smoking is ignoring, and there are no alternative seats. You want to confront him but you are a nervous person and fear causing offence. In other words you have both the external resistance of the situation to contend with plus your own internal resistance with respect to a reluctance towards confronting the person in question. You may not want to move seats for fear of causing offence.

The idea of people not wishing to move seats for fear of causing offence is no trivial example. Such things do happen.

There is no telling how a lack of confidence can manifest itself, particularly in terms of the relationships that people have with themselves and each other.

For instance, consider the fact that some women, at one point in time, did not even have the confidence to change a household plug, simply because it was seen as part of a whole package of activities that were not encouraged for their gender.

Another story that illustrates the point about how a lack of confidence can manifest itself is the following: a friend of mine, who gave me permission to relate this incident, told me that she once went to the park and fell asleep in the soothing heat of the summer sun. When she woke up, quite tentatively, she discovered that some boys playing football were using her as a makeshift goalpost. She became so incapacitated by her embarrassment about this fact that she decided to stay there pretending to be asleep.

Let's approach the question of dealing with the smoking situation from a mental muscle point of view. Again the way we approach the challenge depends on the question: "What can I gain out of this to benefit me?" and "What do I need for myself, with respect to my growth?" It may be that in the first example although there are options open you are the type of person who doesn't like to "cause offence" either by asking a person to extinguish the cigarette or even by removing yourself from the situation. So an identifiable goal might be to ensure wellbeing by not putting up with incidents purely out of feeling embarrassed about confronting them. The aim then is to deal more with your internal resistance by dealing with the resistance that the external situation offers.

It may be the case that you feel that you lack a bit of courage, in which case the person who is smoking next to you presents an ideal opportunity to begin to develop the courage-muscle at a low intensity level. Opportunities to develop this muscle are presented by both scenarios, with scenario 2) offering that bit more resistance because of what might be the deliberate and defiant stance of the person concerned.

If there are no options available and the person won't quit smoking then it might be an idea to change track and ask yourself how this new and increased resistance might serve you. This situation could be valuable if you have decided some way along the line that you need to acquire more patience, tolerance and less irritation. The situation then becomes a relatively lightweight introduction to trying to acquire those qualities by bearing the weight of the irritation.

Besides, on occasion, we each have to learn to let go of that which we want no matter how reasonable, just, or deserved because we know that this world is often anything but just and reasonable. The more opportunities we can have to practice this skill the better.

A person may or may not comply with your wishes. You cannot assume that a person is going to respond exactly the way you want them to. Such a circumstance merely means the intensity of the challenge is increased, and dictates an option; either you can move away (if you have the choice) or you can ask yourself how you can make use of this new situation.

These things must be weighed, commonsensically, into the equation. If a person looks as though they are going to erupt like the top of Mount Fuji on a bad day then keeping quiet might be the sensible option. However, jokes aside even if they don't meet your request at least you made a request which is surely a trophy on the mantle piece for you, especially if it concerns something you feared confronting.

You can always use the increased resistance to assist you in other ways. For instance, if you feel annoyance or anger at the reaction you get from having your request rebuffed you can use this positively to help overcome the initial embarrassment you were feeling about moving seats. In other words you can use it as a means to motivate you.

We sometimes make the mistake of thinking that emotions, like anger, are necessarily bad but it really depends on what you do with them. Furthermore, there is a wealth of difference between using an emotion such as anger and being used by it.

Whatever quality you have decided needs working on you should make it clear to yourself: "I need courage," or "I need patience" as the case may be. You should also make clear the specific nature of the resistance that you need to work with or the "weight" you need to lift, metaphorically speaking. Then you should affirm repeatedly to yourself that by taking whatever action that is reasonable you are preparing the way for greater confidence. This is the thought process that needs to be cultivated. The point of this is to make a heavy impression on the mind of the intention to make a change.

After a decision has been made and action taken it is also wise to reflect on how the situation was handled, and what was achieved overall. Just as I said before, it isn't always the case that an athlete is going to win that coveted first prize just because they have done all the training. But the fact is that they would have gained lots of other things along the way, such as physical strength.

From the point of view of the mental muscle philosophy, if you don't get your way you haven't lost because at least you provided yourself with the opportunity to practise having your say. In the process you have started developing the confidence, through practice, to ask for what you want. And we all know that practice is the forerunner of achievement, which is why athletes train. Above all else, in terms of the focus on the prize, an athlete never knows when today's loss might be implicated in tomorrow's win.

From that point of view you were quite successful. Even the act of trying to meet your need is an achievement in itself. It is so often the case that people with low self-esteem think they have no needs to meet because deep down they think that they don't count. Such actions disprove the case.

I would like to comment further about the use of the smile in this programme for tackling resistance. There is an interesting exercise that we can do with smiling. It is often commented on that where a child breaks into a smile and laughter, at the drop of a hat and at other things more surreal, literally hundreds of times a day, an adult by comparison is lucky if their smile-count breaks into double figures.

More often than not adults wear either a straight face or a scowl. Smiling is a visage that we seem to be ill-at-ease at wearing. It's often the case that we see angry people walking down the road and we don't batter an eyelid, after all, we reason, that is the way life is. Yet if we see someone walking down the road laughing or smiling we somehow jump to the conclusion that they must be deranged. It seems to be anathema for people in this culture to be smiling for no reason. "What have you got to smile about?" is the comment that is often heard.

As adults we forget to smile or have it knocked out of us. Our reliance on smiling becomes less and less until, I believe, our muscles internal (mental) and external (physical) start to become fixed by way of accommodating to a habit of being. In other words what we don't use we lose.

Practising smiling offers an interesting exercise in resistance. Try it for a moment when you find yourself a quiet space where you can be alone. If you are not used to smiling and try to hold a smile beyond what you normally do you will see how difficult it can be; how the face muscles fight to go back to the position they are used to. There comes a point where the lips even start quivering. A similar thing happens when we do an exercise such as press-ups, for instance, and are not used to it. The unaccustomed body sometimes shakes in response.

If you time yourself up to the point when the smile drops, this gives you a level upon which to build. From then on you can practise holding a smile for longer and longer periods. You then have to have time to build up belief in the validity of smiling which is better done in a piecemeal fashion.

This exercise and smiling on the whole can benefit you in a number of ways. In the first place it makes it easier for you to smile more generally and comfortably, I would argue, just as the development of any muscle makes carrying anything, even the body itself, much easier. It makes it easier to slip into a good-humoured mode, rather than irritation or annoyance, because smiling becomes a viable option, or another way out when things get difficult. Just think of people who are able to see the funny side of things as opposed to those who are unable to do so. The former may not have always had this quality but may have learned along the way.

That is why people go to Stand-up Comedy classes so that they can learn to be funny and see the funny side of life. We don't always need a reason to smile. A smile can take on its own justification: and don't forget the mind normally gives feedback to the body about the state it is in by producing appropriate hormones. A good run round the park, for instance, produces feel good hormones called endorphins.

The belief in smiling, humour and laughter as a form of therapy in its own right is becoming increasingly popular these days. It is now being used as a panacea to deal with anything from promoting well being, treating depression, to aiding cancer treatment. Studies are beginning to emerge on the beneficial effects of good humour on the nervous system. An article on injury prevention appearing in the running magazine *Today's Runner* urges us to "smile and keep smiling..."; going on to state that "the happier you are the less likely you are to be injured and the faster you will recover when you are."

The article draws on research from the medical journal *The Lancet* in order to support its claim. This research demonstrated that:

Americans dying of cancer that were given counselling and encouragement lived twice as long as those who got identical medical treatment but without the happy words.[1]

Studies are beginning to show the enormous benefits of smiling on the immune system. According to one article in the *Guardian* by Lizzie Gardner entitled *The Pursuit of Happiness:*

Laughter and pleasurable experiences in humans are known to decrease levels of the stress hormone Cortisol and help fight respiratory complaints by increasing the level of immunoglobulin in our system.[2]

As far as developing mental muscle is concerned, you could even combine the smiling, against the resistance not to smile, with certain circumstance, such as the resistance offered by waiting in a bus queue. This would be for those slightly more advanced than the novice because unless you are someone who can work above the basic level it might be too much of a weight to bear. By choosing the above examples I am merely trying to demonstrate a way that it can work. You have to suit it to your needs.

It is for you to decide the qualities you need to acquire. You might have an irritating boss who takes advantage of you and therefore you use the situation they provide to make yourself assertive by confronting them. On the other hand you might have a shocking temper and therefore spot an opportunity to allow this irritation to help you control it in a gradual fashion.

There is a physical exercise from the world of Tai Chi which may be of use to us here. Tai Chi works very well with the idea of taking in and yielding to other's energy until it becomes necessary, from a defensive point of view to send that energy back. This is embodied, practically, in the exercise called "Push Hands". This involves two people, with hands pushed up against one another in a martial stance. One pushes as far as they can whilst the other allows their hand to be pushed whilst, at the same time, feeling for the opponent-helper's energy. At the point where the person pushes, so far that they extend themselves and therefore dissipate their energy, then it is the turn of the other to push back.

This continues in one long flowing cycle. It is a bit like the riding of a bicycle. One leg pushes whilst the other leg releases its push, or yields, in so doing creating the harmony which results in movement. An interesting question emerges as to which is in the stronger position the one that is pushing or the one that is yielding? Before you come down firmly on the side of the one doing the pushing, don't forget that the one who is pushing will not necessarily feel strength or power if his or her own power is not reflected back through the other's force.

If someone pushes hard onto you and you yield instead of becoming solid like a wall then they are likely to become unstable. Then perhaps it is time to push. The point is that sometimes there can be just as much strength in yielding. What is important is what the need is. Sometimes in life we need to allow ourselves to be pushed and sometimes we need to push. Developing wisdom, another muscle, should help us to know which one we should employ.

A short word on tackling resistance that is thought-based. A lot of the time when you have to deal with challenging thoughts such as worry, anxiety, fear etc they are normally linked to something else in the real world. This means that you have the option of meeting the external resistance that causes such thought disturbance which then has a knock-on effect of diminishing it. On other occasions worry and anxiety may appear unaccompanied. But regardless of where the disturbance comes from you can still take a mental muscle approach.

You can make a start by asking how the resistance of such thoughts can benefit you. One of the answers to the question can be the fact that it can push you in the direction of taking greater control of this region. For instance, this form of internally-situated resistance, in forcing you to train yourself to deal with persistent thoughts, can pave the way for greater peace. With practice, something that is used to deal with such a problem as unwarranted, intrusive thought, initially, can be used to deflect a hungry mind that wants to be fed constantly.

Here are a few tips for coping with mental resistance such as that of worry.

Pleasant thoughts

See how many pleasant thoughts you can call up to obstruct the worrying or intrusive thought. If you are successful for even a second then there is no reason why you can't be successful for two seconds and so on. Obviously with practice you will get better.

Detachment

Try to observe the thought as though you were a spectator watching a piece of theatre taking place on the stage. Try not to interfere or reason with the thought just as you would not interfere with a performance upon the stage. This has the effect of demonstrating that you and your thoughts are not the same: that you don't have to be bullied by their demands. Sometimes thoughts think themselves but we don't have to latch onto them as a child would grab onto a passing balloon.

Introduce a time gap

See whether you can introduce a period of time, when the mind is occupied with something else, between each episode of worry. The idea is to make this period of time grow.

Thought substitution

Instead of thinking in a way that promotes and reinforces a negative position, see if you can substitute it for one that promotes the harmonic conditions you desire. For instance, instead of thinking, "I'm late for my appointment, I've blown all my opportunities out of the water. All my future plans are now ruined. What am I going to do?" Why not try thinking: "I am late but the best thing that I can do is keep calm and think about a way that I can rescue the situation. It is not the end of the world." The first way of thinking is a dead end and merely provides opportunities for building, thought by thought, a house of negativity that will eventually collapse. The second way opens up the mind to the possibility of dealing with the situation effectively.

Be in the moment

All too often our worry relates to the past. If we had our worry a second ago it is already in the past. Why carry it on if we don't have to. I am not saying this is easy. It requires practice but trying to be in the moment, in the here and now can help. The idea is to focus on what is around you. Pick out something external to yourself such as a tree. Look at the people and what they are wearing. Take an interest.

What do you notice outside of yourself? Don't over-analyse in case you just get drawn back into the domain of heavy-duty thought. Sometimes our thoughts like a good scrap with us and over-analysing can provide the perfect opportunity for such a fight.

Before we leave this chapter I would like to make an important distinction at this point between using people and using a situation. There is a vast deal of difference between the two. To manipulate people for our own ends is unethical. To use a situation that leaves you very little room to manoeuvre is intelligent. If you have a choice and you don't have to suffer under the yoke of a situation then don't. If you don't have a choice then you should try to turn the situation to some use or advantage.

I know that people will have more to contend with than simply the resistance of sitting next to a smoker. I was simply trying to demonstrate, by way of example, the methodology and philosophy of dealing with resistance. as a result of trying to deal with some of the situations you will have to face, coupled with this programme, you will be in the process of developing one of the greatest and most useful of mental muscle; that of imagination.

The following boxed list relates to other types of mental muscle that you might want to think about. All are qualities and facets of mind and all can be developed, which make them ideal candidates for the programme of mental muscular development.

See if you can come up with some of your own and add them to the list.

Type of mental muscle

honesty	integrity	empathy	love
daring	boldness	compassion	
frankness	determination	deliberation	
perseverance	sincerity	courage	
patience	understanding	outgoingness	

The following is a list of challenges that are common to human experience and the specific type of mental muscle (in the boxes that could be benefited from tackling them.

Challenge of a dead-end job

Imagination	fortitude	bravery	courage
resourcefulness	passion	learning	challenge

Relationships

Relationships are a great but often wasted opportunity for developing all types of mental muscle.

resolve	openness	understanding
tolerance assertiveness	forgiveness	integrity
negotiation kindness	balance	courage
steadfastness creativity		

Conflict

Conflicts offer many opportunities for developing mental muscle. Here are just a few ideas:

perspective	fairness	negotiation	creativity
humility	yielding	tolerance	balance
courage	fairness	wisdom	responsibility

Personal Injury

None of us like to suffer any form of personal injury. However, such situations present the mind with a lot of opportunities for growth in these ways:

empathy   insight   courage   understanding

awareness   determination

Decision to leave one's homeland

It's never easy for a person to take the decision to leave their homeland and there are many reasons why people take the decision to do so, through choice and otherwise. All the decisions have their own psychological weighting. Here are some of the qualities that can be obtained from confronting this form of resistance.

courage   single-mindedness   mental resolve

determination

Lack of stillness

Sometimes we rush around out of fear of confronting unpleasant aspects of life. We can gain from confronting this tendency in the following ways:

stillness	awareness (of surroundings)	perspective
patience	selflessness	

Even the small things that are a challenge can help. Resisting watching, TV whilst eating, can help to develop one-pointedness or focus.

Bereavement

Facing up to mortality is one of the most challenging things we can ever do. If we choose to take on board the challenge it offers we can find ourselves opening up to gaining all sorts of qualities. Have a think about the following:

fortitude	perseverance	determination	resolve
courage	understanding i.e. (preciousness of life)		

Before we leave this chapter let me just offer a short word on the idea of physical training helping the mind. There are times that when you are in the process of training the body you are also in the process of training your mind. When you decide to go out for a run or pursue a particular activity (at the same time) you also imbue yourself with attitudes such as that of refusing to take the easy route, or becoming a couch potato.

By accepting challenges in sport it can prepare you mentally for accepting challenges per se. The best of the martial arts have recognized this, acknowledging wisely that a person who is disciplined in relation to physical activities also paves the way for cultivating qualities such as confidence and mental fortitude.

Life then, in all its richness, offers so much opportunity for mental gain that can be of benefit to yourself and indirectly to others. All you need is a willingness to catch whatever is thrown at you, or handed to you, and shape it so that it can serve as your liberator rather than as your jailor.

Chapter 4

The Law Of Progressive Resistance

".... 'tis as with Art, wherein special
beauty springeth of obstacles that have been overcome
and to graces transformed; so the lover of life
will make obstructions serve, and from all resistance gain
strength..."

Robert Bridges

Weight lifters, body builders, or indeed any athlete training for strength, will lift progressively heavier weights. They usually do this by way of repetitive exercises which are designed to work the muscle. Endurance athletes such as runners must find the resistance needed to improve endurance and strength. They can do this by adding distance to their exercise regimen or by including increasingly demanding terrain to their training programmes, such as that of steep hills.

The speed of the run may be increased as part of a strategy. This method will also help improve the resilience, efficiency and performance of the cardiovascular system. The cardiovascular system is the heart and lung combination that regulates such activities as blood pressure, and is also responsible for supplying the muscles with oxygen. The more the cardiovascular system is trained the more of a load, in terms of demanding exercise; it will be able to bear.

All this will not be done in an ad hoc fashion but in a highly systematic and progressive way so that the body can obtain maximum benefit. At the same time, the athlete will be able to avoid the burn-out that accompanies dealing with a work load that has not been slowly worked up to.

A dancer, in order to obtain maximum flexibility, will stretch elastic-like muscles in a gradual and systematic fashion. He or she will increasingly push beyond current limits until his or her goal is reached. The human body responds to this resistance, or challenge to its accustomed state, by becoming more flexible accordingly. I like to call this the law of progressive resistance.

What follows from this physiological insight is a clue as to one of the best ways in which to handle the mental challenges that confront us; that is to break the challenge down into manageable elements.

This might seem like an obvious idea, but often people think about dealing with a challenge all in one go, instead of thinking about dealing with it in a form that that will suit their mental strength or limitation. Some people may be able to deal with a challenge in its totality whereas for another that same challenge might cause them to stall because it seems too great.

More often than not, facing up to a big challenge, whether it is in the form of taking a new path or modifying behaviour, can be too overwhelming a task, if carried out in one go. Consider, for example, people whose aim is to give up smoking. Not everyone can give up smoking in one move and stick to the non-smoking regimen.

Such an all-or-nothing approach can be too violent, too sudden or simply too much of a shock for the mind and the body. Consequently, the ex, or not so ex, smoker needs great reserves of mental strength in order to cope with this situation. This strategy can also have the effect of leaving the mind too hungry. As a result, it is all too often the case that the smoker regresses b to the point at which they were before he or she started the regime of immediate exclusion.

This is particularly the case if a new mindset or individual culture, such as one built around increasing general health and wellbeing, has not had time to take route. Crash-dieting, where a person takes up a minimalist diet in order to lose weight is another area where this is clearly demonstrated. All too often, the mental demand coupled with the physiological effect of the diet on the body's metabolism can send a person in the opposite direction: overeating. That is why the side-effect of people starting and stopping an extreme diet of exclusion has given rise to the term yo-yo dieting.

A resistance gradient that facilitates the breaking up of challenges into manageable chunks makes sense. If a massive boulder was stuck in your path and you couldn't just roll it away then it would be wise of you to break it up into manageable pieces with whatever tools you possess. If the fragments end up as pieces of various sizes then there are a number of ways you could deal with them. In the first instance, you could tackle the heaviest first whilst you have lots of initial energy. With this strategy you might run the risk of putting your back out because of the lack of acclimatisation to load-bearing.

On the other hand you could gain more benefit (over time) by starting with the smallest and eventually work your way to the heavier items. The advantage of this strategy is that each successively heavy stone would help to build you up to carry the next, by enabling you to build strength.

I often think that if I had applied the step by step aspect of the mental muscle approach to learning Spanish so may years ago that I would have learned that language by now. Instead I panicked in the face of how much there was to learn. I guess I wanted to learn it immediately instead of piecemeal. Yet I remember the bits that I did take on board so well which means that the language muscle was responding. Now I have gone back to learning Spanish with a new strategy of giving myself bite-sized challenge-chunks to chew on i.e. pronouns one day, adjectives the next. Sometimes we have to pace ourselves and build up to the task. We have to identify what specific things challenge us and then build up to them.

Some of life's challenges then are best faced in a piece-meal way where specific challenges are broken up into separate areas or units of increasing difficulty. Just like for the novice runner the easiest challenges would be done first with the hardest being tackled last.

This has the advantage of allowing the achievement and accomplishment gained in mastering each challenge to facilitate the development of confidence and enthusiasm. Additionally, it also helps to reinforce the, "I can do it" mindset which in turn provides the foundation and drive for tackling the next stage of the challenge. If the achievement at each stage is accompanied by reward such as internal praise – about which I will say more – then, in my opinion, this is a better blueprint for success.

Let's look at a simple example. Reflecting on my days as a student, I remember how difficult it could be for students, myself included, to set about writing essays. The process would go something like this: "I don't know what to write but hey I've got a week: no problem." The week would turn into four days then three then two, then a matter of hours, with the result that either students worked frantically overnight because their back was against the wall or they just cried into their beer.

All this, just because they lost confidence in trying to tackle the essay in one go. It is all very well if you can tackle it one go, just as there are gifted athletes who more easily accommodate to the event for which they specialise. However, if you can't then a method must be found that can help to achieve the goal.

Now I don't want you to simply dismiss this example as trivial. The reason I say this is because in confronting any challenge, large or small, it can come to represent that of a quest, particularly if your confidence isn't very high. By that I mean it is something which tests you and like all good quests can come to stand as allegories or symbols for other things such as the battles you have both with and within yourself. So there are beasties to be slain, dragons to be won over, forbidding landscapes to be negotiated and gold to be found.

That inner terrain has largely been put in place by your life experiences (including that of your education). I once knew a person who was a great writer, as well as a highly intelligent person, but no matter how hard he tried he could never complete his work on time because of the crisis of confidence that overtook him. The problem was remarkably resistant, despite all the reassurances from friend and teacher alike. He stayed on at University for many years but never completed the course. At the time it made me wonder about the type of inner landscape that he had to negotiate and about what experiences had fixed this problem in place.

Because you bring yourself to every challenge then if you are low in confidence, this attitude can come to colour or be reflected in what you feel about your challenge and, in turn, make it appear bigger or smaller accordingly. In some cases it can make you call your whole self or aspects of yourself into question.

Coming back to the essay, I noticed, as did others, that whenever I wanted to finish the essay in one go, it became a massive challenge just to sit at a desk with empty paper. That is what writers block can sometimes be about: a task can loom so large that it begins to take on an inhibiting life of its own. Animated by your own energy and growing anxiety, it can wilfully crush you.

Knowing the task's challenging nature to me, it would have been better if I had taken a mental muscle approach and broken it up into smaller challenges of increasing levels of resistance. For instance, reading for the essay may be the easiest challenge, in which case it would form the first rung of the scale and completing it, the hardest, which would form the last rung. Of course, it all depends on what you personally find easiest, easy, hard and hardest. That is something you must find out, about any task you are faced with.

Then there would be all the grades in-between in order of increasing difficulty. Brainstorming for ideas could come next, followed by putting down one topic-sentence denoting what is going to be in each paragraph, which in turn can be followed by such things as including one-word bullet-points denoting other ideas, or expansions of key ideas in each paragraph. Writing the introduction might be next followed perhaps by writing a paragraph at a time, or even a draft. Depending on the time that is available these tasks can be spaced-out into a time framework that is comfortable.

Each stage is a goal in itself but what is important is that it is a manageable one. It shouldn't be too easy as to make it not worth the challenge; a state of affairs which could leave you feeling short-changed in terms of accomplishment. On the other hand, the task shouldn't be so demanding as to ruin confidence. With enough practice you should be able to manage more loads per task as a consequence of the mental muscle used to dealing with the particular task of essay writing, in this instance, grows.

You have to remember that a weight-trainer would use a weight that is in proportion both to the strength already accumulated as well as to the strength desired. Obviously, there must be balance between the two points otherwise it would prove catastrophic if a weight-trainer tried to lift something way beyond the strength that she or he has. The correct balance is to lift a weight which challenges your strength in order to work a muscle. From a mental muscle point of view the idea is to build up to taking on challenges that are very great.

As an untrained person, or one who isn't naturally predisposed to the event, you may not be up to the challenge of addressing a thousand people in a public-speaking engagement. However, you might be quite capable of rising to the challenge of doing a small lecture, particularly if at the beginning of the challenge-gradient you already have the experience of talking to small groups. This experience would act as a foundation for other challenges. When you are fully accustomed to this level of experience you can then move onto the next. Therefore, you can see an easily definable gradient between your natural qualities, qualifications and skills and the goal or series of challenges leading up to the goal.

A resistance gradient then is simply an elevating line, or scale, which symbolically depicts the following:

- the increasingly difficulty of a set of challenges;
- the increasing intensity of resistance of a challenge or;
- a hierarchy of demands to be met.

One way of thinking of a resistance gradient is as a hill, with all the attendant meaning and metaphors that are inherent in the word hill. The elevation of the hill shows exactly what the challenge entails. By envisaging a hill you can also see quite clearly where the difficult bits are going to be and, therefore, where you might want to take a rest. Hills have another advantage in that they depict progress by telling you how far that you have come, what you have accomplished, as well as how far you have got to go.

You know, as with most hills, that the closer you get to the summit, the steeper it is, and the harder the climb, but by the same token you also know that you are closer to the end. Such knowledge can only help to spur you on. This is similar to a long distance runner who suddenly finds the mental and physical resources to pick up speed because he sees the end in sight.

So a resistance gradient makes it easier to conceptualise the sense of increasing challenge or resistance. The gradient, or hill, is actually scaled; with the scales representing the point of resistance, or areas that are intended for mastery on the way to the end goal. Someone who has been attacked in the street might well have to have a plan of action that steadily builds up confidence. This may entail going out with a helper, to aid the scaffolding of confidence; followed by forays out into the world whose distances gradually increase. Let us now look at and how to construct a resistance gradient.

The main aim of this exercise is to give graphic or visual representation to the resistance that is to be faced. It is not indispensable, but what isn't dispensable is to have a sense of tackling resistance in ever-increasing steps. This will help you to be mindful in not tackling challenges that are too "heavy" for your current psychological state.

For a runner who is building up to running a marathon he will increase his resistance by steadily building up the amount of miles he will add to his regime. He might also increase the resistance for his main goal of say winning or participating in a marathon, by doing some hill-running, training on the sand and/or in the snow or rain.

A runner's resistance gradient (diagrammatically represented) may look like the following:

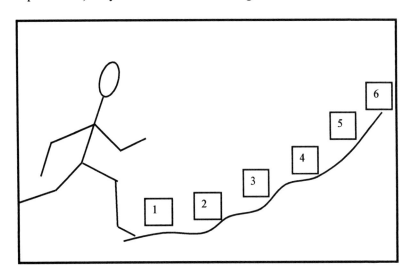

Figure: 2

In the runner's case, the number 1 could stand for the amount of miles that could be run in the first week of training. In the first week, one mile would be attempted. In the second week, two miles would be attempted etc. The numbers are, at one and the same time, challenge points. On the other hand the numbers could merely represent intensity of training. Point 1, to another runner could mean running at moderate speed for two miles. Point 5, could mean running an eight mile session that takes in a couple of big hills. It all depends on the challenges that are being sought which are in turn based on the runner's need.

All serious runners will have some sort of plan for how they are going to improve and make progress through the steady increase of resistance. A plan will help to ensure progress and prevent injury or overexertion. The athletes who often risk injury are the ones who don't have a plan: who haphazardly take on events without any real preparation. For a quick sprint to the shop no training is needed; for a long-hall marathon, preparation is needed. Be warned mental athletes.

Obviously, we don't always come to grief because of the lack of mental training we have but we often don't reach our potential either. Also, think about the times when, with nothing to power us but daring, we took on a major challenge without really thinking it through and ended up on our metaphorical backsides. In this case more was bitten off than could be chewed.

For a person working with weights, a point 1, level challenge might mean working the shoulder muscles, using a bar with 20kgs of weight. A point 2) level challenge could mean doing the same exercise using a bar with 25kgs of weight. This extra increase could be undertaken after a week or two weeks. It all depends on an alliance between the following factors: how strong the person is, how much progress they think they can make and how much progress they would like to make.

The weight-trainer simply begins with the smallest of the weight challenges and trains for strength in order to be able to meet the next challenge on the gradient.

From a mental muscle point of view, the way you would construct a resistance gradient would depend on what your challenge is or what you are trying to tackle that is providing the resistance. It could be your need for courage, a lack of self-belief, standing up to the tyranny of the boss or dealing with low self-esteem. It could be trying to get out of an abusive relationship. The list is endless. Typically, a lot of people suffer from low self-esteem for all manner of reasons, some more obvious than others. Let us see how a resistance gradient might work when applied to low self-esteem.

Firstly, if you are suffering from low self-esteem and you have sufficient insight into the problem, then a note must be made of all the various ways that the low self-esteem is manifesting itself. For instance, low self-esteem could show itself in a difficulty in saying "No" to other people's demands. Additionally, one might find oneself ending up in abusive relationships as a consequence. When the list is made out, the various manifestations should be placed in increasing order of difficulty. Let me repeat the claim that this makes the task of facing the generalised challenge of low self-esteem more manageable.

The following diagram, (Figure: 3) on the next page, is a resistance gradient as applied to low self-esteem. The scales on the line are numbered from one to eleven, depicting the ever-increasing resistance of the various challenges, beginning with the easiest at number one.

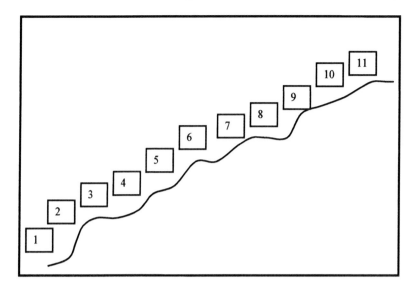

Figure: 3

Here is what the numbers on the scale mean:

1) Continuously lending money out, particularly to people who don't return it.

2) Poor self-image which leaves you constantly criticising the way that you look.

3) Not speaking your mind for fear of disapproval.

4) Seeking approval for your actions instead of seeking to establish whether the actions and decisions meets with your own approval first.

5) Catering for everybody else's needs but your own. Always putting yourself last.

7) Putting yourself down in other people's company.

8) Enduring insults from people with a smile yet deep down taking them to heart.

9) Not putting forward your good points.

10) Denying the value of your feelings. For instance, saying something is alright when it isn't.

11) Reluctance to take up courses or join clubs for fear of embarrassment or due to self-consciousness.

There you have it. All these separate points on the scale amount to a humungous amount of general low self-esteem. As a side note, some of these areas could even be broken down into separate resistance gradients. For example, you might be a person whose self-esteem is basically fine and may not have a difficulty with anything outlined on the list, apart from finding it hard to say no to people's excessive demands; to the detriment of your own well-being.

I am not saying all low self-esteem has the above manifestations, or that they would be put in this order of increasing elevation. This model is only meant to demonstrate how the scaling method works. Each person has to research how the low self-esteem, or other problem, manifests itself for them, just as each athlete would get to know the particular and various ways that their own discipline affects them.

For instance, for one runner undertaking a training routine, one of the hardest parts of the programme that he might have to contend with is actually getting out of bed early in the morning. For another it may be facing the lousy weather, whereas for another the most difficult part might be facing the hills. A third runner might find the last of these to be the best part of the training. You might be a person who has relatively little difficulty taking up courses in which case this challenge would occupy a lower rung on the scale or perhaps it might not even appear on the scale at all.

Similarly, the inability to say "No" as part of a pattern of low self-esteem might occupy different positions of the gradient, depending on what you have to say "No" in relation to. You might find it easy to say "No" to the double-glazing salesperson or unsolicited telephone sales, but you might find it more difficult to turn away the overzealous and pushy caller at your door. Where you place the difficulty in saying "No" can also depend on the proximity of the person to you who is making the demand.

In other words, the resistance may be increased in proportion to the closeness of the person to you. It could prove harder to say "No" to a parent than it is to an old friend. It can also depend on what you feel is at stake for you. Saying "No" to the bosses unreasonable demands might be harder because of practical considerations, such as a fear of job loss, which further complicates your relationship with your self-esteem. Yet it could be precisely the action to take if you want to enhance your self-respect.

You could be a person who is generally fine, as far as your self-esteem is concerned, but for some reason still have a problem resisting other people's excessive demands. If this is the case, then saying "No" can and should warrant a whole gradient all of its own.

When you have constructed your resistance gradient and have outlined the challenges in order of increasing difficulty, then there are certain procedures you can follow, some of which you have already come across. These procedures make up the total approach to tackling internal and external resistance.

What can I get from facing these challenges?

This is a question that should be asked of each challenge on the gradient, or any challenge you have to face. It provides incentive for, as well as supports, the recognition that you can gain something out of adverse situations. You obviously don't want to face something on the basis that their will be nothing to gain at the end of it. Let me remind you that the whole point about why bodybuilders, athletes, and dancers court resistance is to gain something. It is no different with regard to developing mental muscle.

The idea of asking how the challenge can benefit you helps to support the tackling of the challenge. In weightlifting parlance this is called "The Lift". If you know that you are going to get something from a situation that you are going to face, especially if you think it through beforehand, this can give you confidence to confront that very same situation. It is like an athlete taking nutrition in order to provide the body with extra support for the task. It also empowers you by making you an active participant in whatever is happening to you or in and around you.

Let's return to the low self-esteem gradient in order to demonstrate what I mean. In response to the question: "What benefit might I gain from accepting the challenge?" It could be said that what you can gain from each level of challenge is the same thing; namely a cumulative gain in self-respect.

Even when you have tackled a challenge, and your actions don't immediately lead to success, or people frustrate your aims, there still remains the fact that you dared to try, whereas at one stage you dared not. Therefore, you have changed a set of circumstances, both within and outside of yourself, by that simple fact.

With self-respect comes increased self-esteem, if you see your achievement as a valid one. You have proved that you are able to make demands on the world instead of thinking that you exist merely to be the footstool of the people who inhabit it. That is the general answer that comes from asking the question what can I gain from each of the challenges?

But there are also specific gains to be made from each particular challenge. For instance at scale 1, or challenge point 1, (**Continuously lending money out**...) there is obviously the monetary aspect of the gain especially if a door-mat tendency has left you open in the past to not being able to get your money back. I remember when I was a youth and on my first foray abroad. The destination: Paris. I was suffering from chronic low self-esteem, and a shrewd man in a market place ended up selling me a figurine which I didn't want but bought because I didn't know that a word such as "No" existed.

For some strange reason I thought I owed him my time and my money. It felt as though it was my duty to listen to his slick sales patter. Before I could stop myself I had parted with the cash. I even spent a number of hours trying to sell the figurine back to him and to people in the market, generally. That incident was a symbolic representation of my internal state. It taught me a great deal.

At challenge point 5, (**Catering for everybody else's need**...) the gain to be made is independence of thinking; as well as the good feeling that comes with that of becoming your own person. It doesn't mean not consulting with other people ever again. It simply means that you can form your own judgements and opinions, whilst being able to modify them with other people's advice, or input, if and when necessary. It means that you are in the driving seat rather than being a passenger of a vehicle where anybody can take a hold of the wheel: good and bad driver alike.

By confronting the resistance offered by challenge point 5, you can hope to gain more time to devote to yourself. I am not arguing for selfishness here. There is a major difference between doing something for others because you feel responsible, caring, or concerned and doing it because you feel self-hatred or have a low opinion of yourself.

This self-hatred can commit you to being like a feather at the mercy of breeze, with the breeze being that of people's whims. It can also mean that what you offer a gift is not really free at all because if you are at the mercy of something else then it is very hard to act freely.

By facing and overcoming point 7 (**Putting yourself down whilst in the company of others**) what could be gained here is better friendships. It has become common knowledge that sometimes people with low self-esteem attract people who want to capitalise on their vulnerability. It can be as though low self-esteemers exude a certain perfume or smell that attract a predator. It's a bit like those hungry fox's in the cartoons that are attracted to the chickens and a bubble pops up (representing the foxes thoughts) that show a picture of the chickens roasting.

A wily fox that is out to use will spot you very easily; after all, it is its nature. You become fair game. Refusing to do such things as putting yourself down in company leaves you less open to this happening. You will send out a symbolic message to yourself and the world and it is this: "I respect myself enough not to put myself down therefore I expect the same amount of respect from those around me."

Confronting challenge point number 11 (**Reluctance to take up courses**...) potentially opens up a whole new world to you of activities and interests, whether it is sport, an acting class or one where designing or art is involved. For a start there is the pleasure that the activities bring. This pleasure in turn becomes a symbol of your goodwill towards yourself if you can appreciate the significance of the act. Attending classes that ask something of you form a basis on which appreciation can be received within a team setting.

You might participate in acting workshops and be applauded for your efforts. What you design or make can bring with it reward in the form of praise from other course participants, friends or family. Such celebrated achievements can only help to build you up and reinforce an emerging healthy sense of self-esteem, partly by giving you richer experiences.

The final note on the above is that asking how you can benefit from a challenge helps you to bypass the worrying unconstructive mind which might believe challenging situations are hopelessly insurmountable. It is a bright spark in the dark that offers you direction because a reason for facing up to a challenge is found.

At its most basic you will always have gained some sort of knowledge and knowledge is a useful resource for the other situations that you have to face in life. No experience in life is truly wasted; everything can be recycled.

Now that we have had a brief examination of what you can gain from these specific challenges let us now look at the next stage which is an assessment of the skills you possess for tackling these challenges.

Assessment of skills

As I have already mentioned, a good athletics coach, who tutors under a proper training programme, will assess at some point what the athlete's capability is in order to gear the training accordingly. Similarly your starting point should be an assessment of your qualities and skills in accordance with the event towards which you are gearing your training.

As I indicated in an earlier chapter, you should think about the specific challenge and then see if you can draw on either experiences in your past or skills that you possess that can help you to master the challenge. This process will enable you to generate the "I can do it" mindset.

For instance, no matter how low the self-esteem, or how worthless people feel they are, I have never met anyone who has never accomplished anything. They may not acknowledge or be able to acknowledge that which they have accomplished, or it may not be the great achievement they wanted, but it is still an accomplishment and, therefore, is of some use. This world all too readily values the gross and ignores the subtle. A person is seen as being of great value and as having achieved lots just by virtue of appearing on T.V. but what about the person who, in an increasingly materialistic world, just simply looks out for people's welfare for no financial gain?

What an achievement. Success, in my view, is looked at so narrowly that people don't even think they are successful unless they have achieved some sort of fame. Now that is a massive stick against which to not only measure yourself but also to beat yourself when you haven't "succeeded."

An achievement is an achievement whether deemed great or small and all achievements, if acknowledged, can help us, at the very least, to appreciate ourselves a little more and at the very most provide motivational power for pursuing a dream. If you have difficulty saying the word "No," you might look back into the distant past, perhaps even as far back as childhood, and discover a since-forgotten incident when you stubbornly refused to be bullied by someone's demands and did something about it.

There might have been an occasion when somebody dismissed you as useless at some activity, and with this dismissiveness ringing in your ears, you decided to make a success of doing what you were told you could not do.

When you recall some memory of specific achievement you should always try to remember how good it felt. These memories can be drawn upon and the energy extracted out of them like juice sucked from an orange. Don't forget that thoughts are not just idle, inert things, they are powerful units of emotional energy that can either propel you in a positive direction or a negative one. They have "life," so to speak.

You can be walking down the road when you suddenly have a thought about being loved by somebody close to you and find yourself overtaken by an overwhelming warmth and energy.

The reverse is also true of course. You can be overcome by dread which suddenly emerges from the mind. If thoughts and memories can produce energy, then try to cultivate the positive use of them. What better if you can tap into past events that can help you.

One memory that I draw upon from my childhood, which has often sustained me through difficult challenges, is something my mother said to me. I was about seven or eight years old when I decided to clean out the yard at the side of our house. I tidied it to perfection then went inside. I always remember my jam tart reward − my mum used to bake her own − and my mother saying to me "You can do anything once you put your mind to it."

When I am feeling crushed by life and I can care to remember this incident it does me an awful lot of good and I have still retained the memory of the smell of the freshly-baked jam tarts. So although I suffered from low self-esteem and had internal bullying voices telling me that I could never amount to anything at least there was a quiet Tiny-Tim-of-a-voice, slightly drowned out by all the rest, telling me; "You can do anything once you put your mind to it." All I had to do was encourage this voice to become louder. It did.

Sometimes when I am looking for inspiration when having to solve a problem of a practical nature, such as having to move heavy items, I sometimes draw on the memory when I used to be labourer and had to move heavy things and didn't want to risk injury. I remembered the schemes and devices that I used to build out of scraps around me to help.

I got to the point where I believed that I could find anything within the immediate environment to help a situation. It worked without fail. This helped me in turn to engender the idea that where there is imagination there is always a way.

When thinking about your challenges you need to be imaginative: imagination being a muscle in itself that, I believe, grows with exercise.

With reference to challenge point 4, (**Seeking approval for your actions**...) you might find an example(s) of a time perhaps when you consulted yourself in order to make a decision about something instead of deferring it to someone else. It doesn't matter whether the example relates to something big or small. It can still provide motivational inspiration.

With respect to challenge number 5, (**Catering for everybody else's needs**) you might find an example of a time when you decided to do something for yourself for a change. Perhaps you can a recall an episode when you decided to give yourself a treat of some kind; a treat relating to some activity that you don't normally engage in. You may have decided to take yourself for a massage despite the expense.

At the time you might not have looked at this act as significant but it can be seen as such now. Why? Because you sent out a powerful symbolic message to yourself that you intended to look after yourself. Such acts become a signal to the train track operator, in your mind, to move the track so that the train moves in another direction. You should recall how good it felt to do such a thing. Again this is about using the energy that is present in the memory.

Maybe with respect to challenge number 8, (**Enduring insults...with a smile**), instead of enduring an insult you decided to challenge it or gave as good as you got. Everybody has a limit and sometimes, even if it is unconsciously, another more wholesome but shrunken part of ourselves may push us towards rebellion, out of self-protection. We need to be aware of such incidents.

Another point I would like to make is this: when drawing on skills and qualities that will enable you to meet the challenge you face you shouldn't just think about finding specific skills to match specific challenges. Allow me to illustrate what I mean. Imagine that you want to be more outgoing with the opposite sex, but find it hard to do so. You could approach this task in several ways, depending on your experience. If you have one, you can draw on a positive memory of when you approached the person you had your eye on, with nothing to fuel your actions but sheer boldness.

If it worked then that is quite a positive memory to draw emotional and motivational energy from. The other level of experience is that you did the same thing but it was not so positive. Alright, so you did not get what you wanted but the memory is still salvageable. For a start, there is great achievement in acting against your fears in order to pursue what you want. If you don't get what you want this time then you might the next time. It certainly gives you a better chance than someone who doesn't try. The other thing to bear in mind is that life takes everything to dust and with it the bruised ego. You don't want to be sitting in an armchair at the age of one hundred thinking about lost opportunities and of how you wished you had pushed yourself a little more.

What if you have no such memory to draw on? Well you could draw on another level of experience. You could draw on what could be termed a related memory, one, for instance, where you talked to someone, man or woman who was a perfect stranger, for no other motive than to strike up a conversation.

It is not so hard to strike up conversations with strangers providing you feel safe, you approach them in the right way and you respect their space. We all know how it easy it is to get people talking about the things they like to moan about such as the weather or the lateness of public transport. There are some common conversational set pieces that every culture has.

You can also draw on qualities such as determination, guts, feistiness and courage. I don't believe that there is a person alive who hasn't displayed these qualities in some measure no matter how lowly they feel they are. Even to get out of bed when you are feeling low can be an achievement and therefore should not be taken for granted. Within the context of being depressed, it can be heroic indeed.

An athlete doesn't just come equipped with the skill, technique and the tailored physique to compete at their specific event. That is only part of it. They must have spirit, heart and determination.

When Muhammad Ali won the Heavyweight Boxing Champion Of The World title from George Foreman in 1974, after initially being stripped of his title for refusing the draft, do you think that his victory could be put down to just physical skill? No; cunning, guile, determination, pride and resilience were very much a part of his victory.

You have to remember that George Foreman at the time, had a fearsome reputation and Muhammad Ali had been written off by various commentators as someone without a hope in the world. If a boxer is knocked on their backside or a runner comes last, all that may stand between their current loss and future victory may be a dogged determination. And if this is the only thread that is holding up their dream then sometimes, as has been demonstrated by determined individuals, these threads can turn out to be remarkably strong.

Sometimes it is simply a matter of transposing a skill. It is a little like learning to play a piano and coming to the understanding that the tune you played on the piano in one key, or at the low end of a keyboard, can be played at the higher end or even transposed into another key entirely.

It was the Jazz musicians who perfected the habit of taking extracts or "riffs" from other tunes, some of which might have been quite banal such as *Happy Birthday To You,* and added them to musical improvisations, in order to provide anything from humour right through to familiarity for an audience. The Jazz musicians would also learn to play the same tune in many different keys in order to develop greater dexterity, fluidity and skill.

Something that we have all had to do is confront our fear, whether it be the fear of the dark, starting school, potential loss, beginning a new job, or taking a role in a film. There will always be occasion when all of us can recount the successful overcoming of some fear. Now fear often plays a part in the challenges that we face. For example, when we find it hard to say "No" the internal thought underlying part of our stance could be something like, "What response will I provoke if I say "No"? Will the person hit me, get angry with me or even withdraw their love?" "Will I be left feeling guilty as a result of my action, etc?" One thing that we can often gain from confronting our fears is the knowledge that sometimes the fear is not in proportion to the reality of the situation.

After facing up to our fears we often realise that the ground hasn't opened up, consumed us and shuttled us off to hell just because we dared to confront a situation.

Any memories you draw upon to aid you in pursuing your goal, I would ask you to recall in as much detail as possible. This is particularly the case whilst preparing for the big tasks. This is the ideal place for it really. I will also say that by drawing on memories, etc, you are making use of a bigger self rather than just your limited present self you have immediately to hand.

It is a bit like someone who initially tries to change a tyre with bare hands and comes to realise the wealth of resources they have in the boot. Again, with practice, this method of thinking will become easier so that the gap between supplying of usable resources relating to the memory and the task to be performed should lessen. Let us now look at the next stage in building mental muscle.

A Plan of Action

I don't feel that I need to say too much about this. It is always wise to have a simple plan of action when confronting a challenge. This needn't be excessively detailed but just needs to sketch out the steps you will take to achieve your objective. The main advantage of doing so is that it enables you to think through what you are doing. It also acts as a declaration of commitment to spur you on, particularly when your plan is there in writing. Additionally, when planning you can use the research to plug the gaps in what you don't know. This strategy, in turn, can help to engender confidence as well as tame any excess unbridled emotion.

When looking to give up an addiction, for instance, you could get books out from the library on the subject. You might gather useful information about such things as how people learn to master them. On the other hand, you could find out information about what gives rise to cravings and when they are likely to be at their optimum. Books can play the part of an external helper providing you with information, insights and angles that you hadn't thought of.

If you want to get into a relationship you can ask successful couples about how they met, or you could simply just map out the steps or the words you will use to help establish a connection with someone who catches your eye. Part of the preparation could involve giving yourself a positive mantra to recite, about which I shall say more.

Being unprepared, even if it is only to meet the unexpected, can create problems. You only have to read the mind-boggling statistics in the papers to find out how many people have met with accidents through undertaking Do-It-Yourself work on the house. All because they didn't think through what they were going to do and how they were going to do it.

A good athlete, such as the marathon runner, always checks the terrain and plans how she is going to tackle the course. She will look at the points at where she should seek to increase speed and decrease it amongst other things.

Once a plan is completed you can then make use of the following technique to reinforce your resolve to master the challenge.

Mental Rehearsal

Mental rehearsal involves finding a quiet space, taking a few minutes, without interference, to imagine accomplishing that which you actually do want to accomplish in reality. In my younger days I used to go on long runs but before I did so I would instinctively find a quiet moment and visualise the entire course with me running it. I would note the surprising difference it made to my performance. I used to perceive this strategy as akin to almost throwing my imaginary self forward which pulled my actual or real self along in real time.

It wasonly when I grew older that I realised that people developed similar techniques for employment in areas such as sport and meditation. I also came to recognise that these techniques went by different names. One name being that of Creative Visualisation. Hypnosis itself is just another variant on the same theme.

Rehearsing, mentally, works in similar fashion to the way that an actor or actress might rehearse for a play, but not only just to get the play right. It seems that judging by some accounts mental rehearsal has more benefits than just preparing a person for an activity or boosting confidence. Rather, in some mysterious way, the technique's power maybe analogous to a person building a kind of engine which helps to propel them towards success.

A simple example of mental rehearsal is the way that musicians will mentally play their instruments whilst looking over a piece of written music before they play it in order that they will be able to play it through without mistake.

There is also the reverse side to this ability of the mind to be motivated by strong imagery and thinking. Sometimes we seemingly prime ourselves for disaster due to intense negative thinking in relation to an event; with predicable results. Self-fulfilling prophecy is what we usually call it. We repeat, to ourselves, a mantra that we are going to fail, which in turn helps us to visualise this failure and surprise, surprise, we actually do fail.

Even in the field of athletics the benefits of such techniques as visualisation and mental rehearsal have not gone unmissed, and are becoming a large part of an athlete's training repertoire. Athletes now attest to such ruses as running a race inside their heads, so to speak, before they run the race for real.

The following technique is the simplest form of mental rehearsal. Once you have found a quiet spot, place yourself in a chair or on a bed and make yourself as comfortable as possible. Then you need to encourage your whole body to relax. This can be best achieved by a method of systematically letting go of any tension in any parts of the body. Any good relaxation technique could be used here.

The next part of the process is to visualise acting out the behaviour that you wish to promote in a mental scene that is as close to reality as possible. In other words the scene must be like real life in all its detail but also, just as importantly, so should you. If your goal is to address a number of people in a lecture it is no good imagining yourselves as Martin Luther King or Rosa Luxembourg on the basis that they were good speech makers.

If you are meeting a challenge that demands courage there is no point in envisioning yourself as a hero or heroine from a Marvel comic complete with cape and extraordinary powers. The scene has to retain truthfulness. Again this is where the planning can help you.

Visualise yourself succeeding in doing what you set out to do. This is why performers such as Stand-up Comics set great store by checking out a venue in which they are going to perform. It is a way of mentally priming themselves and getting a feel for what the atmosphere will be like, so that they can secure a power base within it.

Let me issue a word of caution. It doesn't mean that because you visualise success that when you do it for real the entire escapade will be problem-free or a success. Life offers no guarantees of success in any field, and sometimes for good reason. You could be rejected for that one place, e.g., a particular university you set your heart on and worked so hard to get into. However, this does not mean that your actions were a failure. It just means that someone else put other obstacles in the way, in so doing providing further resistance.

As far as you have done what you have set out to do, then your endeavours have been a success and you can be proud of yourself, particularly if the challenge is something that you never would have attempted before. I, for one, don't really believe in "failure", because you never know when the event giving rise to the F-word will be implicated in some future accomplishment as I made clear in the first chapter . It is very important not to have this sense of having failed. Your endeavour is a platform that can be used for building experiences that can be of much use to you.

Besides, sometimes I think we place too much emphasis on that external trophy at the expense of overlooking the internal trophy that we have won.

A good optional extra, is to offer yourself words of encouragement whilst visualising the meeting of the challenge. You can use phrases such as the following:

"I can win over this challenge."

"Just the fact that I can attempt to overcome the challenge shows how much I have grown in strength." You can make up your own mantras to suit the purpose or get someone to help you develop them if you like.

The development of positive encouragement and affirmations has further relevance. I am of the view that all people have a subliminal core philosophy or mantra (repeated phrase) that betrays their attitude towards themselves. These mantras are like music that plays in the background, just below the level of awareness. We occasionally take notice of these mantras because we recognize the tune or because it suddenly gets louder. If you listen carefully, you can hear the "I'm-no-good-at-anything" type of person whistling their theme song constantly, as much as you can hear the "I-can-do-anything" type of person whistling theirs.

The mantra can be general or specific. In other words it could be one set mantra that lies in readiness for all manner of situations or it could be one that comes out in response to a particular situation. An example of the former could be: "Whatever is thrown at me I am confident that I will be able to cope with it." The reverse of this may be: "My life is always falling to pieces."

We could be quite confident people, generally, with a healthy core philosophy but all of a sudden when a relationship fails, up pops the mantra, "I am never any good at relationships."

It doesn't matter if your relationships have been unsuccessful hitherto. What you don't want is a negative core philosophy that reinforces the situation by becoming self-fulfilling. How about a core philosophy that says" I know that my relationships haven't been too good, up to now, but with a little bit of work I know they can get better."

Here are John Syer and Christopher Connolly, writing in *Sporting Body Sporting Mind,* making the case for negative attitudes having a detrimental affect on what might be termed the positive self image muscle as regards sports:

> Some of the most deep-seated and stubborn attitudes are the ones we develop about ourselves. If ever there were self-fulfilling prophecies they are the ones which run: 'I can never drive properly when the pressure is on.', or 'I've always taken a long time to get warmed up.[1]

This is why this aspect of the exercise is useful in getting you to try to build a positive core philosophy. Think again of Muhammad Ali and his "I am the greatest," mantra, one which, both reflected and reinforced his position as a champion. Syer and Conolly go on to say that, "A positive self-image is one of the most important and yet vulnerable assets that we can possess....Your self-image reflects the sum total of your experience, thoughts and emotions. It is something which deserves considerable attention and gentle development. "[2]

A positive mental attitude is certainly worth cultivating. Here is a story about how it can really reap rewards in a collective setting. Stories abound about the Manchester United team who became the first team to win the football treble of FA Cup, League Cup and European Champion's League Cup in 1999. Their esprit de corps involved a refusal to say die and, true to this philosophy, United won the Champions League final in stunning fashion. One nil down with only a few minutes to go they scored two goals in quick succession during extra time.

This has more to do with a trained mental attitude that has been handed down through the club culture. It is something they demonstrated time and time again throughout many a season. Manchester United's nurturing of the never say die attitude follows all the pattern of the development of mental muscle. This is what captaining teams, and having team mottos and esprit de corps is all about; getting people to attune themselves to the winning philosophy of the team.

Celebration

Another important part of this programme that should be brought into play, when a challenge has been met, is that of celebration. Let me first start by asking why we celebrate anything. One reason why we celebrate any victory might have to do with cementing new found confidence. Celebrating victories casts in symbolic stone that which has been achieved. Whether the achievement belongs to that of the individual, the team or the nation these achievements can become the potential foundations for the unshakeable building up of confidence which in turn can lead to more greatness.

Whenever you achieve anything you should find some way of registering the importance of the achievement. Whether you deem the achievement small or large is irrelevant because, let me remind you once again, you don't always have the foresight to know how the small or the large will play a part in the unfolding of the story that is your life.

Celebration can run a whole range of gestures, activities and symbols. At its simplest it could mean saying to yourself, "Well done"; anywhere between once and a hundred times. It could mean putting a note in large letters on the wall saying "I did it", which reminds you of your achievement every time that you walk into a room. It could be a treat of some kind, like a visit to a movie.

Ideally, you should try to match your celebration in proportion to the strength of the challenge you have met; saving the best reward for overcoming the most difficult challenge. The point about this exercise is to make the victory significant; to mark it in some way.

Celebrating also helps you to both internalise the victory as well as promote and shore up another emerging image of yourself, just as steel reinforcers will help provide stability to an emerging building. This in turn can go some way towards making sure that you don't retain negative images of yourself.

It is one thing to have a realistic image of who you are but retaining negative images is an entirely different thing altogether. For a start, fixed negative images don't contain the prospect of allowing you to be something different, they merely perpetuate the bad things you feel about yourself.

How often do we come across people, who, when they are feeling low, have a strange way of not being able to note any achievement in their life. The only mantra they seem to be repeating in various ways throughout the conversation is "I'm a failure." You say to them:

"What about that time when you tackled that stampeding herd of Elephants single handed?" and they say something like;

"But I didn't stop them stepping on the grass, I'm a failure."

"Yeh, but what about that time you climbed that mountain and rescued that cat," and they go on and repeat the mantra and after two hours you are getting ready to tear your hair out. I don't wish to make light of this condition. I'm just exaggerating to make a point. It can be a serious problem for some people who sometimes can see no goodness, whatsoever, either in themselves or in what they have achieved. I should know. I was one such person. Their mental muscle, concerned with self-esteem certainly needs working on.

Achievements become all too readily lost if you don't give them recognition by celebrating them. It is like denying the sun to a plant that you are trying to nurture. Finally, celebrating helps provide the impetus and the confidence for tackling the next challenge. That is one of the main reasons that I place a great deal of emphasis on celebrating achievements.

The helper

What can you do when your challenges become all too heavy: when you have to carry what seems to be too much weight to carry on your own? There is, in weight-training culture, a way of training that involves the use of a "spotter" or "helper." When a person wants to lift a heavy load, slightly beyond or almost out of range of their strength, and for the purposes of really pushing themselves, then often they will enlist the aid of a friend or training partner known as a spotter or helper.

In this case the helper will assist the person in a variety of ways. For instance, he might simply stand by and watch to make sure that the lift is made safely; getting ready to step in if a heavy lift goes wrong. I have known it happen whereby a person has carried out a heavy lift to exercise the chest area but the weight has come down on them and for want of another presence they have ended up injured.

A helper can also assist the person in making the lift by taking hold of the bar in order to stabilize it; only letting it go once the person doing the lifting has the bar firmly under control. The helper can also aid a partner by helping then to exhaust their limits by urging them on. A helper may assist by bearing the weight of part or the entire bar, particularly after the person doing the lifting has really exerted themselves to the point where they can't produce anymore effort. Basically, the helper can assist in any variety of ways and at any point in the process

There is something of use to us in the concept of the helper. Namely, that what you find difficult to deal with about a challenge you can enlist the friend or a helper for. You should generally try to do as much as you can for yourself but you can also seek help for the aspects that you find difficult to deal with or lift; metaphorically speaking.

It could be that you just want someone to hear you out or bear witness to what you are doing. You might want a helper to give you encouragement or you might want them to step in and offer practical assistance at a certain stage. For instance, you might be able to cope better with the challenge of going to night school if someone can help with looking after the children. On the other hand, you might need someone to help you check over your written work, if it is not your strong point. The helper could even be a counsellor or therapist who can give extra guidance or support.

Decide what you need the helper for, and try to enlist his or her help for the specific task. However, try to ensure that they don't end up doing all of the carrying otherwise you won't grow. Don't let someone who is good at writing write all your essays when they should only be checking yours over. It is your challenge so own it.

Inform your helper about the "load" that you are going to carry and what you would like their role to be in helping you with this load. I made use of a helper when I was preparing to perform in a one-person show which I had written myself. This was at a time when I was struggling with my confidence. My particular helper helped me to build up the "I can do it" mindset by exploring with me all the skills I knew I possessed, which would enable me to achieve my goal. My helper also reminded me to enjoy what I was going to do.

I reinforced this process further by posting comments on my wall that related to positive comments I had attracted for other performance-related work. It worked. As soon as I took to the stage I found that although feeling a little nervous – a state I could make use of to charge the performance with energy – I also felt a profound peace.

And if I needed further proof that you can test for the presence of mental muscle by the mind's capacity to handle more of a load, I found that from that point on, it was easier take to the stage and perform other one-person shows without even the need for a helper. I even learned to make use the resistance of fear. Instead of trying to bury it, or waste energy fighting with it, I went along with it and used it to give emotional edge to my performance. It became, in this instant, my servant rather than master.

Another variation on the helper theme which is suitable for some situations is that of the absent one. The absent helper is useful from the point of view that if you can't get someone to be with you in actuality you get them to be with you in "spirit" so to speak. I like to call this one, "carrying your love in your back pocket."

If you have to confront a situation that makes you quite fearful sometimes it can help if you carry a picture of a loved one. If you don't have a photograph you can simply have them in mind. Imagine them offering you love and encouragement as you undertake your task. I recall a variation of this being useful to someone who used to suffer from panic attacks.

All true friends root for us and want us to succeed in what we do. However, we often don't know how to carry this love or support with us as, though it were the latest scent, so that it can prop us up if and when we need the help. New lovers seem to do it in some way. You see them walking down the street all twinkle-eyed and to them the world and all its problems seem to just melt away with their every embrace.

Having people root for us in general is crucial. It gives us a sense of validation. It is like the athlete getting spurred on by the roar of the crowd. This is the reason why some athletes, such as track athletes, positively stoke up the crowd before they undertake their event. Muhammad Ali did this to good effect when facing one of the toughest fights of his entire career; against George Foreman in Zimbabwe; the famed "Rumble in the Jungle" fight. He would whirl his fist in motion as though stoking an imaginary fire and get the crowd to chant a mantra verging on a war-cry.

A further variation is to have a mental picture of someone whom you admire, or you could read a biography of theirs. The point of the exercise is to find someone to act as a symbol for the direction in which you wish to proceed or the qualities which you wish to pursue or embody. Such a person could symbolise courage, peace, stubbornness, tenacity, or triumph in the face of "failure" etc.

It is not for nothing that 60's radicals had posters of Che Guevara on their walls during the 1970's. A favourite poster of would-be martial artists and others, during the same period, was that of Bruce Lee. For some people, to think of Nelson Mandela, who was locked in a prison for twenty seven years for fighting against apartheid in South Africa, is to bring up images of courage and forgiveness etc.

The story of Evelyn Glennie, as told in her autobiography *Good Vibrations* contains a great deal that is of interest to the mental athlete. Evelyn Glennie made history by becoming the world's first virtuoso percussionist. Her achievement is made all the more remarkable by the fact that she happens to be deaf.

The first signs of deafness appeared when she was aged eight. As her hearing grew worse she faced the prospect of having to attend a school for the deaf and give up on her studies in percussion. However, she refused to accept an imposed limitation. It was said of her that she was "always enthusiastic to master anything that appeared to offer a challenge."[3]

Glennie noted that as her determination grew so too did her confidence. In so doing she went on to master many percussive instruments in spite of the doubters. Her positive mental image of herself was as a percussionist that happened to be deaf and not as a deaf percussionist.

On overcoming the challenges that ensured her success she said, "I was determined to get the best out of every opportunity that came my way and to do my utmost to win through the obstacles." Also within the book, Glennie acknowledges her debt of gratitude to significant persons who both believed in and supported her. Again this shows the importance of the "roar of the crowd" egging us on: the helper who helps us to lift those mental weights.[4]

Another area that is worth considering as a mental helper are stories about mountains and the people who climb them. Mountains have always held a fascination for people and have become a spiritual metaphor: usually for the trials and journeys of the human "soul". They appear in many stories and myths. For instance, in *Lord of the Rings*. The challenge that a mountain offers easily translates into a direct symbol of human endurance, perseverance, fortitude, resilience, courage and triumph.

Keep a diary

It is good to keep a diary or some sort of record. Athletes usually keep a diary. Within its pages they include such things as sizes of developing muscles, training carried out, cardiovascular output, miles run and weights lifted. At its most basic it is a record of progress. Similarly as a mental athlete you will also be able to chart your progress by keeping a diary or some sort of record. Your diary can also document what more there is to do as well as how your confidence is coming along. You can even add little notes regarding the need for such things as alterations in your training. The diary can also be used as a means of reflection.

You can use it to explore what you gained from tackling the challenges you faced. The more you aid yourself in looking at the benefits the more benefits you will be able to find even if you weren't wholly "successful" in getting a result from trying to master your challenge.

The more you practice looking for the benefits the better you get at it or the bigger the muscle grows. This in turn provides further incentives for facing challenges. Keeping a diary is a way of measuring strength. It is a mental tape measure for reckoning the way that you are growing or more precisely your consciousness.

Because the diary is your personal statement of development and is therefore, by definition, something special, you could invest in a nice little book. This would be a statement in itself; one which will come to symbolise your willingness to take yourself seriously.

Let's return to a consideration of the purpose and usefulness of the resistance gradient. A resistance gradient is something that you can either write down or with practice keep in your head. At its simplest it helps to separate the various challenges that constitute a major challenge so that you don't freeze in fear at the enormity of it. The resistance gradient can be used as a basis for tackling all sorts of dilemmas, small and large. As long as there are things in the world which resist us in our quest for general and individual well-being and inner peace then the gradient can be used to confront them.

There are two periods in my life relating to low self-esteem where the unconscious use of the resistance gradient worked for me. One example is that at one stage in my life I felt almost incapacitated with an episode of feeling quite low in spirit. The temptation I had was to run away from myself, to find something to earth it in. I decided then to believe less in the strength of this feeling and more in my own strength, which I intuited, I could steadily accumulate.

Every time I had an attack, I invested a steadily increasing amount of time that I would spend just being with it before rushing off for support. That way I came to reinforce my own strength. Additionally, I was beginning to overcome a "learned helplessness" that suggested that I could do nothing for myself. I grew stronger through reinforcing my sense of power rather than powerlessness.

I am not discouraging people from seeking help. Seeking help is a very good thing, and it is a great pity that some people actually feel ashamed about needing it. That mindset has got to change. Rather, I am I am trying to put across the idea that seeking help can be accompanied by an investigation and promotion of one's own power. As somebody who has shared a seat with depression, I know that that depression is often reinforced by the feeling that you are powerless, whether in the face of life or in the face of your own emotion.

Let's look at symbolism in this regard. Symbolism is an all too important but neglected area. Sometimes the little things speak volumes to us and carry great power. Deciding to sit still, amidst a massive emotional wave that threatens to drown you, is a huge symbol of growing power; if it can be appreciated.

Another instance of how a novice use of the resistance gradient came to my benefit was in the following incident: when I was going to school in the 1970's a concerned teacher brought to my realisation that I had a habit, due to lack of confidence I discovered, of not being able look people directly in the eyes. I didn't realise it until it was pointed out to me that I would circumnavigate the whole of a person's face; without really looking at them; in fact looking everywhere but in their eyes. The teacher, Mr Gallagher would say, "You've got to try develop your confidence, try and look at me."

I simply couldn't no matter how hard I tried. When I got older I decided to consciously and deliberately work on this challenge, partly as a symbol of raising my confidence. I did this to good effect by systematically challenging myself to both look directly in people's eyes and to maintain contact for increasingly longer periods. I didn't quite notice the systematic nature of the process until I reflected on it at a later period of time.

Sometimes we don't readily appreciate the fact that we have arrived at a position of some growth or internal strength in a systematic way. We take it for granted that that is the way things are or have always been so we don't see the joins or the process. But if we make a closer examination we might see the process.

The following is a quick summary of the procedure for building mental muscle.

- Form a resistance gradient
- Review similar challenges already faced and use your knowledge as a resource.
- Review or list the skills that you already have which can be used for tackling the situation or challenge.
- Ask yourself how the challenge can benefit you.
- Have a plan of action.
- Rehearse mentally.

- Celebrate achievements after meeting the challenge.
- Keep a diary of your progress.

Chapter 5

Muscles Worth Developing

"The real joy [of victory] is the joy of sharing it with our friends."

Yannick Noah (former French Tennis Champion)

Following on from my starting point, it now becomes obvious that there are a myriad varieties of mental muscle; some more obvious than others. There is the confidence muscle, the humour muscle, the self-esteem muscle, in other words aspects of mental activities, processes and qualities that can be trained, developed and enhanced.

As long as there are qualities, there are muscles to go with them. In this chapter I would like to highlight a few that I think are worth developing which concern the sympathetic relationship we have with our inner life, with others and between ourselves and the environment. For what use is all that strength if it merely exists as a self-serving vehicle? Human beings are social animals after all. The beauty of such an event as the Olympic Games, representing the culmination of physical development and performance, is that it is a world event; one which can benefit us all.

Yet, there are other spin-offs that can cascade from the individual quest for athletic perfection to the general populace, such as what is learned about endurance and fortitude as well as about advances in nutritional science. There are similar things that we can learn from mental athletes.

The best-that-we-can-do muscle

For the purposes of general mental strength and discipline, it is always worthwhile doing tasks to the best of our ability. Far too often in today's modern culture we have a tendency to do tasks well only in terms of whether we are going to be paid well or rewarded. Gone are the days, by and large when a task was worth performing for its own sake. A true test of integrity is whether a person can perform consistently with the same regard for a task regardless of whether payment is involved.

There are some of us who are beginning to hold dear to the principle that money, as well as other things material, are the only issues that really talk. It never seems to occur to us that sometimes the most rewarding payback comes from doing something in the best spirit.

A similar thing can be said in relation to the current state of athletics, and soccer which demonstrates how pervasive this way of seeing things has become. Where once it was everything to be able to play for one's team or represent one's country now the overriding motivation seems to be that of money or status.

It is no coincidence that often when football teams drop a division the well paid stars leave, thus demonstrating the point that when status (and money) is lost then there is nothing else to hold them to the club. Trying to regain a promotion in this age of high finance is not seen as a good enough reason for loyalty.

If you train yourself to do things well when there is no immediate gain then it prepares you (and your mind) all the more for being able to do things very well when it comes to the things that you do like, because you will become practised at giving of your best. A quality such as this and others such as self-discipline can be transferred easily to other areas of life. You will then not only have the motivation born of the enthusiasm that comes with pursuing your interest but also a cultivated self-motivation that can work in your favour; particularly useful if or when your interest begins to wane.

I am not arguing for perfectionism here. In some respects perfectionism can be a near pathological quality where a person constantly measures themselves against some unknown quantity that can never be manifested, and, more often than not, only succeeds in creating anxiety. Nor am I arguing that people should put up with boring jobs or anything that may cause them pain or damage. Anything of that nature needs to be challenged quite vehemently. I am just talking about the benefits of doing our best with the tasks that confront us.

Sometimes we have to do things well that we don't like doing, things that we may consider boring. Yet these things are essential for general mental training; for giving us all round fortitude. It's a bit like an athlete training in wet weather for the extra strength that the resistance of such conditions can bring. It is probably the case that not all athletes like training because it is hard and demanding. They may only like the specific occasions when the crowd is spurring them on.

However, they still need to graft at the less glamorous aspects in order to be able to get the best out of themselves. Think of the athlete who can only perform to his or her best ability when he or she feels enthusiastic. What happens if 80% of the time he or she doesn't feel enthusiastic at all? Another way to look at the issue is to see every aspect of life as dry run, a practice session preparing us for a time when we can do the things we truly want to do. And if not that, then a time when we are going through a difficult period and need every ounce of self-discipline that we can muster. As the great athlete, actor and martial artist Bruce Lee stated:

"To be able to do the things we want sometimes requires the performance of a few we don't. ...Remember my friend that it is not what happens that counts, but how you react to them.

Your mental attitude determines what you make of it, either a stepping stone or a stumbling block."[1]

We ordinary mortals also need to do well when there is no crowd cheering for us or urging us on. In other words at times when we can't readily see the benefit. Sometimes we perform tasks half-heartedly in order that we might take the easy route, or we might try to find the short cut the whole time. This to me creates a mindset that in some cases can be disastrous for us and others. We only have to think of the amount of accidents that occur because people weren't disciplined enough to make the effort to ensure some procedure was safe. How many times do you see people jumping a red light just because they couldn't be bothered to do the right thing.

Short-cutters are the mental equivalent of people who cheat at weights (meaning they perform the particular exercises inadequately by throwing a weight rather than letting the muscle lift it in isolation). They fail to feed the muscle properly and as a consequence fail to gain any strength. The only thing that is fed and grows is their vanity.

Poor training, mentally speaking, is the physiological equivalent of developing a habit of poor posture. If you let your muscle lapse generally it doesn't become good for general things. This is why people sometimes put their backs out by simply doing a little bit of shopping.

The best-we-can-be muscle

This is of great benefit to everyone as well as the planet. We tend to take each other and the rest of the world for granted and fail to treat all things as though they were an end in themselves. Our culture promotes this way through its treatment of all things (human and non-human alike) as a commodity and then people wonder why someone can get attacked for a pair of training shoes.

The question worth asking ourselves is whether the only time we practise being aware is when there is some vantage to gained. Is the only time we take an interest in the environment when our neighbour's overgrown shrub is blocking our view of the sun, yet spend half our time throwing down litter and polluting the atmosphere? So what about the rest of it? Can we really be said to be "good people" in one area whist neglecting other areas. Can we really even love one if we haven't even practised loving all. What about when that "one" love becomes as ordinary as the rest?

The issue I find most interesting, is that if you ask people what would be one of their most horrible nightmares, I am sure that a lot of them would say that it was being alone in the world. Yet by and large we continue to treat people and other sentient beings as though they were simply an extension of our own needs.

This connection-to-other-people-muscle is very much diminished and is in need of some form of invigoration or stimulation, and this takes practice. How can we feel connected to all things in a spiritual sense if we take no care to connect with all things in a practical and psychological sense, treating them as though they weren't a part of us?

To fail in this respect makes a mockery of all religions and ethics. When a car driver knocks down a cyclist, gets out of his vehicle and begins to voice worries over the effects of the collision on the paintwork of his car rather than the person on the floor then we have a culture that is in trouble. I have known this to happen.

If we train ourselves to love more, cultivate greater sensitivity, to become more aware, to be more tolerant, then we get better and more accomplished at acquiring what are just social skills. When we hear people say: "Look after number one, only," then this statement reflects just another form of (poor) mental training with regard to others. Whilst it is judicious to look after and out for ourselves we need to think about whether sometimes this is at the expense of everybody else. If the environment suffers as a result of car owners in rich countries then it obviously is at everybody else's expense.

The trouble is that people don't always set about trying to train these muscles. They may do it on the rebound because they might have done someone some harm in a moment of selfishness and therefore realised that some work needs doing. However, it is comforting to know that even the most atrophied muscles, with regard to these skills, can be trained. All it takes is a little persistence and dedicated effort. Leopards might not change their spots but people do change their ways, for all manner of reasons. With regard to where the planet is at the moment we certainly need to change our ways.

The comparison is with that of the marathon runner who, out of the blue, tries to run a marathon having ignored all those opportunities to engage in small training session. On the surface the missed sessions seem insignificant, but when added together add to the loss of a greatly enhanced performance.

For instance, how much more difficult is it going to be for a person who gets irritated at the drop of a hat to walk away when somebody deliberately winds them up, as opposed to the person who, although she might get irritated, is more able to deal with the source of her irritation because of the way she has taught herself to handle everything else. The point is one has trained for their particular event and the other has not.

The small acts we commit against people as individuals acts as a symbol and paves the way for how we treat them generally. Perhaps we should treat people and all things as though they were us.

Mental Muscle and the Internal Career Ladder.

One of the key challenges that we face is the one of mastering the internal world and strengthening ourselves in the process. This world, with its own set of trials and tribulations demands that we pay attention to it and nourish it, lest its needs leak out unconsciously into the outer world in order to find expression. This is nowhere more apparent than in people's quest for power and domination, be it with respect to people, other living things or the environment.

There are people, in key positions of power, who are not as powerful on the inside as the powerful positions they occupy in the real world. Because their internal insecurity is not addressed they simply usurp more power to fill in the gap.

Often the way they make up for their internal lack is to wield power over others, without justification and often with dire consequences. Hitler is one obvious example. The poem that Shelley wrote entitled *Ozymandias;* about the pathetic boaster who lays everything to rack and ruin because of an unfettered quest for power, might well be a fitting ode to people operating in this mode of consciousness. What is worthy of note in the poem is the ruins that Ozymandias's rampant ego has made to the land, and its people, which he used to rule. The irony of the words written on "a trunkless leg of stone" is worth noting here:

" 'My name is Ozymandias, king of kings:
Look on my works ye mighty, and despair!' "

The words are given added poignancy when we are told that:

"Nothing beside remains. Round the decay
 Of that colossal wreck, boundless and bare
The lone and level sands stretch far away."[2]

It is very important to tackle one's own quest for power. If this is never tackled at source, by making oneself strong internally − the battle in part being to become content within oneself − then the hunger is never satisfied. The power-hungry never take what I like to refer to as the internal career path where, armed with a developing understanding of self, an individual tries to progress to the point of self-mastery. They want to be boss externally but they can't even be boss internally in terms of mastering their wants and their needs.

Like psychic vampires they merely continue to consume individuals. They never seem to realise that it is more powerful to be in command of oneself − a difficult task at the best of times − than to be in command of tens, hundreds, and millions and still continue to feel small. Nobody can hide for long behind a blanket of adulation; sooner or later it simply suffocates them. Besides, that shadow self, composed of all those insecurities, simply follows them around and continues to grow and lengthen as the sun sets on their power.

Hitler, for all his so-called might, didn't even have the strength, courage or decency to face up to the carnage he had wreaked upon the world. Only true strength can allow you to do that.

Allow me ask you a question. Imagine that a very powerful magician said to you that she could grant you the power to either have everything you wanted, but with no guarantee of happiness, or the means of being truly, psychologically and emotionally content. Which option would you choose? And no, you can't get round the problem by saying that I'd take the option where I can have everything and share it with everybody.

If you would choose the latter option then this raises a question as to why our lottery games are solely based on giving people vast amounts of money. Why aren't our psychologists helping to design games where the winner gets a chance to win contentment. That's one game show I am sure that a lot of people would go on.

A wholesome self is the real trophy that must be won. When we win over ourselves, we tend to need less and less of what can sometimes be the tarnished trappings of this world, and come to want more of what we actually need. We also become more available to offer service to this world when it needs us. When the plate from which we eat is full then we cannot help but want to share, with others, that which we do not need.

This is why I think it is important to try to strengthen ourselves mentally. The first rung on the ladder of understanding is the appreciation that much of the excessive hunger that leads us to want to control others can be satisfied internally. When we at least try to either find the origin of the hunger, or do something about it, it is at this point that we can most benefit others. It is at this point we will see the development of true benign power and begin to recognise that true power, and greatness therefore, washes the feet of the people and not the other way round.

The way-of-seeing muscle

One of the questions that concern me from a mental muscle point of view is whether we can develop our perception of the world in order that we can live more off what we see and less off what we have. I am not talking here of seeing no poverty where there is none, for instance, but simply being able to truly *see* and appreciate that which is around us so that we might come to depend less on what is often the tarnished baubles of life, in my opinion.

Can a ray of sunlight, straining through the branches of a tree, come to be more important to all of us rather than the next item that we can buy as fashion accessory? We only seem to take notice of that which is around us when we are about to lose it or no longer have access to it. Losing sight of what matters has come to be like an epidemic that has been steadily taking hold of increasingly younger generations.

I am reminded of a number of incidents when teaching secondary school children who, to their minds, obtained status and kudos from the fact that they possessed a mobile phone. This was at the time when the use of mobile phones was beginning to spread. Both my colleagues and I were surprised by the amount of children who actually felt as though they were worthless without a phone. The phone seemed to become an external symbol of their internal loss of esteem.

This trend played itself out in an incident where one boy put another down, savagely, on the basis that the one under attack had a pager, which as far as his attacker was concerned, was inferior to the phone that he possessed. The boy using the pager was inferior by implication. Now if something such as a mobile can be so charged with meaning that it can affect how someone feels then why can't other more "important" things be so impregnated with qualities that make people feel good about themselves.

These are children who seem less and less to be able to live for the delight of nature-inspired games such as conkers or for the joy of seeing the helicopter-like seeds falling from the Sycamore Tree. For a good deal of children I have taught, you tell them of such things, and you are merely seen as an ageing hippie who is out of touch. What they have is an outward symbol of their power and status. At the same time what is lacking is an emphasis on what they can feel, think and empathise with; in effect what they can be.

I am convinced that we have a limitless capacity to strengthen ourselves internally and to make the tiny things give us pleasure. We can bring things into vision which have the ability to give us the strength, fortitude and the joy that we need. Do we really need to be millionaires before we can be happy? If the answer is yes then it is not because the world is naturally like that but because we have allowed it to become that way.

There is an old Zen folk tale that helps to clarify the point a little more about the implications that our manufactured way of seeing the world has on everything ranging from joy to peace. Are you sitting comfortably? Then I shall begin.

One day an old monk was sat in a one-room house of simple construction. The monk's way of life was quite humble and he had no possessions or furniture to boast of. Whilst he was sitting meditating on the sight of visage of the moon, a burglar entered his property hoping to find things of worth that he could steal. He found nothing except the monk in the middle of the room. The burglar asked the monk whether he had anything to give him. The monk replied that he had no other possessions except for the clothes on his back. The burglar demanded that he hand these over.

The monk complied without fuss or anger. The burglar ran off and the monk returned to the middle of the floor and began once again to meditate on the moon. As he did so he said to himself, "I wish I could have given him this beautiful moon." For the monk seeing came before the possessing. It meant that he could get most of that which he needed to satisfy his internal life from being able to perceive the deeper significance of the external world in relation to his internal world. He simply worked hard on strengthening his spiritual muscle.

Our way of seeing the world is firmly attached to our way of being. The corollary of all this, of course, is that the being of modern people is so consumption-based that we find it difficult to see things outside of our consumption frame of reference.

John Berger says in *Ways of Seeing* that "It is seeing which establishes our place in the surrounding world....The way we see things in the world is affected by what we know or what we believe."[3]

If we are told subliminally (through such media as advertising) which often sells back to us our dreams and longings in a distorted form, or by a cynical society that we are worthless (other than through what we own), then this is going to cause us real problems in terms of how we see both the world and ourselves.

If we are told that things such as phones and cars and other assorted items makes us worthy then is it any wonder than we see the "real" beauty in these things and not in ourselves. Yet it is this very same self that gave the products the power which they have come to have over us in the first place. The value that things have is what we lend to them.

Gold only has primacy of importance over, in some cases, life itself, because we have given it this power by collective (in many cases not so collective) consent. However, we continue to live life as though it were otherwise. Consequently, all we are doing is creating generations of wounded people who find it hard to locate their own intrinsic value. The result is growing disaffection and anger.

As regards our vision and perception, in physiological terms, we often adjust the focus of the eyes, through the eye muscles, in order to bring objects into focus. If you put a pencil in front of your eyes, then focus on it to give it clarity, the background suddenly becomes blurred as it goes out of focus and vice versa. Whichever of these remains in focus depends on whichever you see as important.

There is a psychological and spiritual counterpart to this. It is reflected in the way that we can bring certain aspects of either our internal or external world or both, into or out of focus, with attendant consequences. I recall hearing an ex-member of the Kray gang, who were responsible for bringing gangland terror to certain parts of London in the 1960's, talking about his past. He recounted how he became transformed and how that transformation to a different way of being was all bound up with the new way in which he began to see the world.

He talked about how, at one stage in his life, he was almost animal-like in his cruelty towards people. And then in near-poetic terms described how certain ways in which he began to envisage life became the catalyst for change and what he regarded as his true "rehabilitation." He recounted how he became awestruck with birds "taking sand baths", and these same birds feeding their young with tireless devotion.

He started to see a "beauty" that had never before been part of his life. He noted the season's effects on the trees and how they lost their foliage in autumn but in turn recovered them. He then realised that nature's theme of regeneration could be applied to people with regard to their qualities. It was only a short step from here to his realisation that whatever he had lost or never had he could either get back or obtain, respectively.

Like Saul on the road to Damascus it dawned upon him that he could be something else. He managed to swap his materialistic people-as-commodities way of seeing the world for a more "spiritual" one where life and people mattered for their own sake. In other words he developed the spiritual side of his mental muscle.[4]

How easy is it to recalibrate our mental and spiritual vision, in order that we can appreciate the small things in life, in the same way that we might (re)focus a pair of binoculars in order that we can see things more clearly?

Can we make a glass of water taste good as a Dom Perignon 1302 without having to be dying of thirst in a desert? Can a leaf falling from a tree or a smile from someone who doesn't normally do so be made to be as exciting as a win on the horses? It can to some people; mental athletes, who have either trained themselves or for whom this way of seeing has come naturally.

This is where we can learn from our fellow athletes. I firmly believe that if this culture is to survive with any degree of humanity then this is the sort of road that we are all going to have to take.

We invest the things in the world with meaning which has consequences for what we get out of the things around us. Importantly, we also scaffold children's investiture of meaning in the things around them. You can often come across examples in schools. For example, where children have been awarded a sticker for something they have achieved and think that the sticker is most fantastic thing in the world because it has been invested with the symbolic meaning that it is important.

On the other hand, in other circumstances, they can be given all sorts of expensive things that end up abused, simply because they contain no meaning for them. When a relatively new born child would rather play with the wrapping paper, rather than the toy which it had encased, then that tells us something about the way they learn to invest meaning in the toy as a plaything.

This may offer a clue as to why there are so many more angry children, in England at least, being aggressive and "happy slapping". Perhaps the reliance on consumption has so divested the world of any meaning and any useful rites of passage – such as those that could symbolise their entry into the adult world or test their warriorship and service to the community – that there is nothing much left other than the "big game" of using others as prey.

I came across this story in the press which demonstrated the point further. It was written by Lizzie Gardner and entitled *The Pursuit of Happiness.* In the article she made mention of the fact of how she suffered from depression and how, using a technique that was similar to the mental muscle programme, she taught herself how to enjoy the things in life that some of us may take for granted or perhaps overlook. She mentioned such things as the simple delight to be gained from "clean cotton sheets." Additionally she wrote:

> I'm moving onto achievements next and will slowly work my way up to blowing my own trumpet.... I'm learning to look out for enjoyment in my day. I practice and reward myself by working towards small goals with the incentives that work for me; I

do the hoovering and win Desert Island Disc, a cup
of tea and a fig roll, for instance.[5]

The interesting point about the way that we see the world,
in a physiological sense, is that it is learned, rather than being a
given state of affairs, when we are born. What we see out there
in the world is due to a cultured negotiation between brain, eye
and object. Similarly, the way that we "see" spiritually our place
in the world and the importance of other things to ourselves is, I
would argue, mostly learned.

This is despite the fact that scientists are busy trying to
suggest otherwise by blaming everything on our genes. If you
think I am wrong about what I have just said then think about
other cultures and their differing relationships with themselves
and the land. Indigenous peoples past and present make for
fascinating studies, in this respect, as does the ancient lore of
Western culture.

Towards the finishing Line

Whatever our station in life one factor that commonly links us all
is the unstoppable move towards death; the ultimate finishing
line for all mental athletes if you like. It may be sad but this does
not stop us from using this fact positively. The closer we get to
the finishing line the more we should be able to jettison the
things that don't matter.

When we finally break through that ribbon that separates
one mode of existence from something else or perhaps nothing
else, depending on your belief, one thing remains clear; all that
has been good and bad about life including all that we ever
worried about will be reduced to so much cosmic dust to be
blown about the universe.

This is one of the features of death: it takes the good and
the bad. However, we can treat this fact positively and it can

help us to live life very positively. Knowing this, we can ask ourselves how much of the flotsam and jetsam of life that drifts up to our psychic shoreline are really worth worrying about.

Instead of running away from the thought of death, in its own way, ironically enough, such an end can have its place in helping us to find peace whilst we live. Life and death are the ultimate Yin and Yang. These two colossal, cosmic forces stand in massive opposition to each other, yet they work together to make life vibrant.

When having to confront such realities, often the response from most people is, "I don't want to know." I believe that this attitude is a mistake. By taking this attitude we are cutting ourselves off from a balancing force. Not only that but we enable death to become a big shadow that creates overcast on the light of our lives.

By moving our thought toward death, only slightly on occasion, it can help us to separate the truly important from the trivial. Such a way of thinking shouldn't be a big stick with which we beat ourselves into morbidity – far from it – more akin to a tuning fork with which we are able to test how much we are vibrating in sympathy with the things that matter, such as living things and the planet.

Let me refer you back to the Yin and Yang symbol (Figure 1 in the first chapter). The small circle with the opposite colour to the section it occupies can represent the minor introduction of some balancing element that maintains harmony; just as a drop of bitter medicine might be introduced to the sweetness we prefer, in order maintain our wellbeing. In this case death is a tincture to our lopsided perspective which prevents us from seeing the important: It can be a prick in the overblown bubble of our rampant ego; a cautionary voice that tells us to be careful as we try to bet all our chips at the roulette table of opportunity, or the tap on the shoulder on behalf of the hungry as we attempt to boast of our affluence.

We should use this knowledge to live fuller lives. When we put things in perspective – in light of the fact that we will one day run our last race – it can help us enormously with all the challenges we face. For instance, that physical feature of yourself that you keep trying to hide hoping nobody sees but everybody does by virtue of the fact that you keep on trying to hide it. You can try hiding it less and less and see if you can get to the end point of actually being proud of it.

On that note, it may seem strange but we fare better if we try to own the so-called less exciting features of ourselves. Somehow or other it is an expression of who we are. Just as lines on the face are manuscripts telling its own story about a person's important experience. We have to remember that people personally "disfigure" or alter their appearance themselves, whether it is in the form of piercing, tattoos or embossing of the skin, as an expression of individuality.

Although, granted, there is a big difference between someone choosing something to do to their body and having something like an injury happen to their body. In the latter the element of choice has been taken away. Having said that, it doesn't mean to say that there aren't those amongst us with enough mental muscle to own and use the experience just as Peg Leg Bates, mentioned in the introduction, used his to his advantage.

It is not for me to say exactly how you can or should see things; I am only trying to point out that there are alternative ways of seeing things that others have explored.

This verse from Shakespeare's Cymbeline illustrates, beautifully, the wisdom and judiciousness as well as the advantage to be gained from packing away worry and fear as we learn to be aware of the finishing line:

> Fear no more the heat o' the sun,
> Nor the furious winter's rages;
> Thou thy worldly task hast done.

Home art gone and ta' en thy wages.
Golden lads and girls all must,
As chimney-sweepers come to dust. [6]

Tranquillity

When we set about trying to achieve a state, such as tranquillity, then many aspects of life can come to pose as a means of resistance. This is even true of the positive aspects such as excitement. One end goal might be to try to find an inner core that is peaceful and relaxed, despite all that is going on around us; the rough and the smooth; the good and the bad; the up and the down. Ideally, we need to create a situation where, referring once again to the Yin Yang symbol, we become the entire circle rather than the sum of its revolving parts: in other words we try to rise above the contradictions, or surf them at the very least.

I don't believe that we need necessarily detach ourselves to accomplish this; especially if we open our minds and ourselves to life's challenges. I'll give you an example of what I mean by this. One summer I found myself on a Greek Island. For a laugh I decided to participate in a particular leisure activity that involved being attached to a parachute whilst being towed along by a speedboat. I'm not proud of it, I was bored.

Whilst I was still on board the boat, the ride was fast, bumpy, exhilarating and anxiety-inducing. All the ingredients you would associate with excitement really. The ride supervisors began to wind the parachute out with me attached to it. I became slowly detached from the boat; its frantic undulations as well as the noise from the engine. Eventually, I was up in the sky experiencing so much peace, as the seas warm breeze took care of the parachute. I felt so much tranquillity, yet I was not entirely disconnected from what was taking place below. .

Perhaps we can find peace despite life's undulations. Far from negating and fearing life's resistance, we can at least try to use it to create the breeze that can take us aloft, whilst leaving us connected. Take a concrete example; the bills that come through the door. It would be nice not to have them but do they have to stress us out?

At any one time, given the full range of human potential, people in similar income situations can have an attitude towards them which can range from worry to extreme disregard. The differing response, from individual to individual, might be governed or determined by nothing more than an internal philosophy or set of beliefs.

The best philosophy would be one that enables us to foster a relationship that helps us to not let the bills trouble us whilst at the same time remaining connected enough to them in order to deal with them.

We can call this, if you like a state of attached detachment or detached attachment; a term representing a unity of opposites: meaning attached enough to be connected but detached enough not to have one's inner peace destroyed.

I accept the point that when you don't have money a bill entering the house takes on an extra weight accordingly. Nevertheless, until a way can be found to change material circumstances, we still need to find a way to not be bullied by such an event, and work with the resistance that it offers.

Mental athletes

We are all mental athletes, of one type or another, who from the point of view of managing life's challenges, run the range from the not so fit to the super fit; depending on the event. Let's look to those people who excel at their event, to teach us; particularly those who make contribution to such endeavours as human beings' search for peace and alleviation of suffering. If they love well, treat others well, or they have good understanding then let's borrow some of their technique.

Let's look to good all-rounder like the multi-skilled decathletes that they are, but not in a spirit of following but from a point of view of emulating. We know people can change and grow and develop any qualities, all despite the prevailing trend towards punishment, rather than rehabilitation, as reflected in our penal systems.

As a teacher, I have witnessed the horror of some children who seem to carry with them violence and destruction as easily as they carry their coats and bags. On the other hand I have also gone on to witness the dramatic metamorphosis of those same children into much more positive people as they, with support, have gone on to develop one or other aspects of their mental muscles; previously left flagging. The classroom is only a microcosm of the world: a mini society that responds to the influences of a good coach.

We should, I believe, also look to develop a system which can support the elite social athletes who care about the world and all it contains, the givers rather than the takers for instance, as well as the ones who wish to take up such events but are currently scared off by the world's hostility.

How often have we heard someone's offer to give very human assistance to some cause, being met with, "Look after number one," or "It's a dog eat dog world: who cares." Yet whilst educationalists and psychologists ponder about the reasons why people are becoming so violent, and depressed, they might care to examine the hidden language that is a mirror of a society that has a long way to go in terms of demonstrating it really cares more about its people, than its products or its wars.

The millennium marker, in my opinion, was a great opportunity, missed, for the world to concentrate on moving more seriously towards justice and peace. It was our "high bar," something for us to focus on in a mood of stillness and reflection before vaulting over; in order to land on a soft cushion of enhanced peace, greater cooperation and a more focused tackling of environmental issues and poverty. Instead, we missed the bar completely; only to land on the hard asphalt reality of a war in Iraq.

Athletes set great store by preparing themselves for years to give of their best at major landmark events, such as the Olympics. There is no reason why, on a world stage level, that attempts could not have been made for using the occasion of the millennium for securing more peace in the world, instead of investing the world's hope in costly buildings. How about erecting structures that live forever in the hearts of people?

If one thing children are good it is the act of picking up languages. They learn to pick up very early on the language of *being* within a society, such that they can tell you that you are a sucker if you are trusting or demonstrate responsibility. This is the new song many of them have started to sing.

Just as Olympic athletes, who suffer from lack of funding or institutional support, tend to perform less well overall, despite their natural ability; there are people in this society who could make enormous and positive benefits to people's lives. They often don't, because institutions which reflect the general society's descent into greed and cynicism also treats them with, at the least, a lack of support or, at the most, outright contempt.

If our political systems aren't at their best nor will the people be because the latter will come to be a reflection of the former. One example of this is that we have programmes on the television, – "Reality T.V." –that invite us to be jeering voyeurs of people's pain. This is the modern-day equivalent of putting people in stocks instead of really helping them to alleviate their suffering.

We have indeed moved further way from being our brother's and sister's "keeper" to being merely the watcher of their suffering. When we have finished throwing our collective cabbages bought from the *I'm Better Than You*, store then we might care to reflect on this ritual attack. It all helps to weaken the collective and positive mental muscle.

Whatever happened to the idea, "Many hands make light work." Doesn't this apply to the mental and spiritual spheres as well as the physical?

We are social beings who, at heart, seek companionship, which is as fundamental to our spiritual side as food and water is to our physical side. We don't seem to live a life which resonates fully in harmony with this fact.

What I have sought to demonstrate is that at the point at which you are challenged you are confronted by a door. That door stands between you and growth on the other side. There is a door between a smile and a frown, between an act of peace and an act of aggression, between selfishness and kindness, insight and ignorance, bitterness and a wholesome outlook, low self-esteem and confidence.

You, with a little help from your friends, and a good system of support, can fashion a key that will help you to move from one point to the other wherein the promise of transformation resides.

It is as simple as that. All you need do is foster an attitude or willingness to step through. This is as true for the collective as it is for the individual. There are some real benefits that await you on the other side as long as you rise to the spirit of the challenge and refuse to see challenges as a problem, and therefore as something that is necessarily negative.

The fact that I have written this book or performed in two one-person shows, despite growing up with a chronic lack of self-confidence, I credit in no small part to this philosophy and programme. There have been other forces as well, and that is where my helpers and training come into the picture.

The mind, that allows us to feel so much pain, is also the same mind that provides us with the basis for not only overcoming it or making positive use of it but for creating ourselves anew. Just as something as wondrous and reflective of light as a diamond, evolves out of something as mundane as carbon, so too can we transform both our inner and outer world into the wondrous.

From this vantage point, in the hands of a master craftsperson, resistance (be it in the shape of the lost job, bereavement or injury) becomes nothing more than a tool for cutting and shaping the rough gem. Life's minor irritations provide the means for its polishing.

Note from the author

I am conducting ongoing research into the use of Mental Muscle as well as the question of how challenges are met. This is in keeping with the ultimate aim of Grounded Vision which is to produce and promote works that enable people to foster positive relationships with themselves, others and their environment. If you have any interesting stories to tell about meeting challenges, as a result of working with this book or otherwise, I would be most interested in hearing from you. You can contact me at the following address:

Tony Pryce
Grounded Vision
P. O. Box 42087

Forthcoming events include a website that highlights the positive use of mental muscle as well as people-positive action, so watch this space.

Introduction

[1] Harry Lorayne *How to Develop a Super Power Memory p117*
[2] Noel Entwisle, *Understanding Classroom Behaviour* page 7
[3] Frank Rusty E, *TAP : The Greatest Tap Dance Stars and their Stories 1900 -1955 pp48-50*
[4] Doreen Trust, *Overcoming Disfigurement,* p162

Chapter 1

[1] Stephen Fuller, *Ginseng*: *The Magical Herb of the East,p42*
[2] Ian Ridley *Tony Adams, Addicted*
[3] Dennis Potter, *Writing for Dear Life pp1-2*
[4] Doreen Trust, *Overcoming Disfigurement* p108

Chapter 2

[1] John Syler, Christopher Conolly *Sporting Body: Sporting Mind* p13
[2] Atkinson Rita L, Atkinson Richard C, Smith Edward E, Hilgard Ernest R. *Introduction to Psychology, p665*
[3] Elaine Aron, *Highly Sensitive Person* p51
[4] Ronald Melzack, *The Puzzle of Pain,* p21
[5] Ronald Melzack *Phantom Limbs*
[6] Daily Mirror June 1st 1999

Chapter 3

[1] Alma Thomas *Mind Running*, Today's Runner pp45-49
[2] Lizzie Gardner *the Pursuit of Happiness*

Chapter 4

[1] John Syler; Christopher Connolly, *Sporting Body, Sporting Mind* p106
[2] John Syler; Christopher Connolly, p106
[3] Evelyn Glennie *Good Vibrations* p56
[4] Evelyn Glennie p117

Chapter 5

[1] Striking Thoughts Bruce Lee, p99.
[2] Ozymandias, Shelley,
[3] John Berger, *Ways of Seeing* p7
[4] Channel 4 Productions, *Reggie* 17/2/200
[5] Lizzie Gardner *The Pursuit of Happiness*
[6] William Shakespeare *Cymberlene: Illustrated Stratford Shakespeare*

Lorayne, Harry; *How to Develop a Super power Memory*, Thorsons/ Harper Collins, London 1993

Berger, John: *Ways of Seeing*, Penguin, USA, 1977

Melzack Ronald, *The Puzzle of Pain,* 2nd Ed, Penguin, New York, 1973

Fuller Stephen, *Ginseng: The Magical Herb of the East*, 2nd Ed, Thorsons, England, 1988

Rusty Frank, E. *Tap: The Greatest Tap Dance Stars and their Stories 1900 -1955*, Da Capo Press, New York 1990

Syler John; Connolly Christopher, *Sporting Body, Sporting Mind - An Athlete's Guide to Mental Training*, 3rd Ed, Simon and Schuster, England 1998

Aron Elaine N. *The Highly Sensitive Person: How to Thrive When the World Overwhelms You*, Thorsons/ Harper Collins, USA, 1999

Glennie, Evelyn, *Good Vibrations; My Autobiography*, Evelyn Glennie, Hutchinson, Britain 1990

Chevalier Jean, Gheegrant Alain, translated by Buchannan - Brown, John, *A Dictionary of Symbols* 4th ed, Penguin, London 1996

Entwistle, Noel, *Understanding Classroom Behaviour*, Hodder and Stoughton, Great Britain, 1990

Melzack Ronald, *Phantom Limbs*, Scientific American, April 1992

Potter Dennis, *"Writing for Dear Life,"* Observer: the review, Sunday 31st March 1996 pp1-2

Satorius Dr Dhyan, *" 'Waah - uuuh' - The Best Medicine,"* Hopwood Beverley. The Independent, Tuesday 18th June, 1991

Shelley, Percy Bysshe, *Ozymandias,* Selected Poems, 2nd Ed, Humphrey Milford, London, 1921

Trust Doreen*, Overcoming Disfigurement*, Thorsons, England, 1986

Channel 4 Films, *Reggie* Year 2000

Atkinson Rita L, Atkinson Richard C, Smith Edward E, Hilgard Ernest R. *Introduction to Psychology* 9th edition Harcourt Brace Jovanovich, USA,1985

Thomas Alma *Mind Running: Relax, Run Free and Beat Your Stress*, Today's Runner, July 1996 pp 45-49

Gardner Lizzie, *The Pursuit of Happiness, Guardian 24th April 2000*

Daily Mirror June 1st 1999

Shakespeare William, *The Illustrated Stratford Shakespeare,* Chancellor Press, London, 1982

Ridley, Ian, *Tony Adams: Addicted,* Collins Willow, London 1998

Lee Bruce, *Striking Thoughts: Bruce Lee's wisdom for daily living,* Little, John (editor) Tuttle Publishing, USA, 2000

Aronson Elliot, The Social Animal, 3rd Edition, W.H. Freeman and Company, USA, 1980